THE ROAD

— through the —

DESERT

Text copyright © Alison Jacobs 2001
The author asserts the moral right
to be identified as the author of this work

Published by
The Bible Reading Fellowship
First Floor, Elsfield Hall
15–17 Elsfield Way, Oxford OX2 8FG
ISBN 1 84101 138 X

First published 2001
10 9 8 7 6 5 4 3 2 1 0
All rights reserved

Acknowledgments
Scripture quotations are taken from the Holy Bible, New International
Version, copyright © 1973, 1978, 1984 by International Bible Society, are
used by permission of Hodder & Stoughton Limited. All rights reserved.
'NIV' is a registered trademark of International Bible Society. UK trademark
number 1448790.

A catalogue record for this book is available from the British Library

Printed and bound in Great Britain by
Omnia Books Limited, Glasgow

THE ROAD
through the
DESERT

ALISON JACOBS

MAKING SENSE OF WILDERNESS TIMES

For my parents,
Revd J. Courtenay and Mary Jacobs

CONTENTS

CHAPTER 1

CROSSING THE RED SEA

Read Exodus 14.

Do you ever get annoyed with the phrase 'wilderness spirituality' because the wilderness is somewhere you want to get out of, not into? Do you find yourself stuck in a place that is dry and dull? Do you feel that there is something missing in your life, or even that you are dying inside? If so, read on.

This is not a book about 'wilderness spirituality'—voluntary with-drawal into an empty place in order to meet God. It is about what you might call 'exile spirituality', about finding yourself somewhere you do not want to be and looking for God in that situation. It is about wilderness as prison rather than as liberation—yet strangely enough, liberation may still be found there.

Problems

'Exile' is a situation in which many people find themselves, for many different reasons—some spiritual, some secular. Some are to do with the modern way of life, some common to every age. Unemployment has blighted many people's lives today. It erodes their self-esteem, leaving them feeling worthless, purposeless and—let's face it—bored. Yet instead of sympathy they might find hostility, worst of all in the places where they should expect to get help—the DSS and the church.

People in dead-end jobs can feel similarly. You might be working long hours doing a pointless, thankless job for less than a living wage. And it is even worse if you have previously spent months unemployed, thinking that any job at all would be better than none. Because you do now have a job, perhaps even a safe and steady one, other people think that your problems are solved.

And then there is love. There are whole industries based around the problems of love, from agony aunts to songwriters, but that does not help much if you are the one with the problems. Death and desertion both bring heartbreak, but there is also the quiet despair of those who cannot find someone to love them in the first place and begin to wonder if there is anything about them to love. That situation may be particularly common in the church, where many young women take seriously Paul's advice not to be 'mismatched with unbelievers' (2 Corinthians 6:14). There simply are not enough young men in the church to go round.

Any close relationship can bring great joy or great sadness. Affection that is not returned, betrayal of friendship, or a simple breakdown in communication, can cause years of sadness. Falling for the same person as your best friend, a chance remark taken the wrong way, or one person not supplying help the other thinks they should —anything that is seriously important to us can also thrust us into the wilderness if it goes wrong. One of the worst situations can be if someone we love is suffering and we can do nothing about it.

Perhaps the church itself is the problem. It can be hard to admit but, truth be told, she does not always behave like the Bride of Christ —or even his Girlfriend. We expect to receive love, fellowship and comfort when we need them, but the fact is that many Christians can find the church, either as an institution or a group of individuals, to be a real pain. Bureaucracy, backbiting and fixed ideas can cause untold hassles and be a real barrier to meeting God. When my non-

Christian friends discuss why they are not Christians, the behaviour of people who claim that name comes up as one of the most common reasons. Those of us in the church might want to defend it but sometimes we have to agree with the critics.

There can be thousands of reasons why people feel lost and alone, but it can happen without any discernible reason. A general sense of malaise seems to be growing more and more common—in the words of the Carpenters, 'Rainy days and Mondays always get me down.' 'Being British' doesn't help—by which I mean the tendency to bottle things up, not wanting to cause a fuss or to bother people. I guess that other nations have their own exacerbating character traits.

But what can be done about these problems, this sense of exile? What does God want done about it? This is certainly not the 'life in abundance' that Jesus promised (John 10:10).

Solutions?

This book is not going to provide you with all the answers. I do not have all the answers and I would not trust anyone who said they did. So if you are looking for a twelve-step plan for getting out of the desert that is currently your life, turn back now. If, on the other hand, you are looking for ideas, perhaps I can help.

What this book is about is *exploring* the wilderness—accepting it, learning from it and then trying to find a way out. It is based around the book of Exodus—but not the action-packed Moses/Pharaoh/plagues storyline so beloved of film-makers. They leave off just as the real trouble is about to start. But that is where this book begins, with the years that the Israelites spent going round and round in circles before they finally made it to the Promised Land—their experience of being stuck in the desert.

Most of the chapters are based around individual incidents in Exodus and the books surrounding it. I have not looked at these incidents in the way someone writing a commentary might do, searching out the latest scholarly wisdom or studying a passage verse by verse. That is a very important job but it does not belong here. Instead I have looked at the story and tried to understand some of the things it might be saying, particularly things relevant to the exile experience. This is something like the 'literary' approach that has become popular over the last ten or fifteen years, but in many respects it is the way preachers have been looking at the text for as long as there has been a text to look at—a kind of imaginative speculation.

Most of the incidents took place before the Israelites were condemned to their forty-year wanderings after messing things up the first time they reached Jericho. That is because nothing much happened to them afterwards, which is sort of the point. But you cannot really write a book about nothing at all happening.

There will also be plenty of references to other parts of the Bible, to people in similar circumstances—because there were lots of them. The most obvious example is the thousands exiled to Babylon. The people were taken *en masse*, although some high-status individuals, such as Daniel and his friends, stand out: we all know that being rich or high-born is no guarantee of having a good life.

These exiles left in a group and can speak for a group. Others were lonelier. Hagar was cast out with only her son Ishmael for company. Cain wandered alone. Job did not go far geographically, only to the town rubbish dump, but in some ways he is the loneliest of all— among people, but separated from them by their lack of understanding.

Some of these people brought trouble on themselves; some were entirely innocent. Their broad range of problems, and the causes of the problems, echo those found in the modern world. Society might have changed but in many ways their lives were like ours—although most of them were in a far worse plight than we will ever be. So if they survived and even thrived, I do not see why we cannot. God is as much with us as he was with them, though we sometimes forget it. Perhaps they forgot too—I expect they did—but we have the advantage of living after Jesus, the ultimate revelation of God's love.

9

Jesus

Jesus is very relevant to this theme. He knows exile. I am not thinking here about the forty days he spent in the Judean desert at the beginning of his ministry (although this might be an echo of the Exodus theme). That experience fits better into conventional 'wilderness spirituality'—leaving behind the company of humans in order to talk with God. What I am thinking of is the incarnation itself.

We do not often think about the effect that being born as a human would have had on the divine Word. The idea seems to have occurred only to a few Christmas carol writers (Christina Rossetti in the second verse of 'In the Bleak Midwinter', for example), but I suspect the nearest we could get is to imagine ourselves suddenly reborn as an ant. Or an amoeba. And then some.

Of course, unlike most exiles, Jesus undertook the incarnation voluntarily for our sakes, but that cannot have made it much easier. What must it have been like for him to be confined to one time and place when he created all times and places? What must it have been like to fear death, in the Garden of Gethsemane, when he was 'from everlasting to everlasting'? Or to have been totally alone on the cross when he was one person of the Trinity? We can hardly begin to imagine. But Jesus knows how we feel. God knows what it is like to be in exile, odd as that may sound, because Jesus took his humanity up into the Trinity when he ascended. So Jesus runs through the entirety of this book, even when he is not specifically mentioned. His is the guiding light.

In the two thousand years since Christ, his followers have often found themselves in literal and metaphorical exile, from John the writer of Revelation on Patmos, while the Bible as we know it was still being formed, right up to the present day. To be alienated from others at some point can be an automatic result of being a Christian. We are supposed to be 'in the world but not of it' (see John 17:14–16), even if we sometimes feel that we are of it but not in it. Either way, we are in good company. And that is something to remember: we are in company. No matter how it looks, there are many, many people feeling alienated—Christians, atheists and people of every shade of belief.

And I am one of them.

About the author (and why it's relevant)

I am currently at that indeterminate age—between 'young' and 'middle-aged'; I have been a Christian all my life and have been through a variety of the normal traumas and doldrums that contribute to the exile experience. I have had boyfriend problems (mostly *lack of* boyfriend problems). I have been unemployed for months at a time and I have done dead-end jobs. I mean, I hate waitressing! I know some people really enjoy it but I am just not cut out for it. I've also worked in a perfume-packing factory. I won't say that this is the most pointless job in the world but it comes close. One type took two whole production lines to pack—with inserts, heat-sealed cellophane, the lot. We knew it was a cheap brand, but one morning someone turned up at work saying that they had seen it on sale locally... for £1.49 a bottle. That did not make me feel good about my work.

All this was a few years ago.

One thing I had known since I was a child was that God wanted me to be ordained. It was not what I wanted—no way. I tried putting it off but in the long run I was prepared to go along with it. He is God, after all. I got through to the second stage of the candidating procedure for the Methodist ministry, before being turned down flat for reasons that were never explained to me in a form that I could understand.

That was hard. It meant a thorough re-examination of my call. But that experience is not why I am currently in exile, though I do believe it contributed. The real crunch came a month later.

I got a cold. We were away on a long weekend in London, it was freezing and I got a cold. A week later, the cold was better but I was much worse. Three months later, I was diagnosed as having ME. That was seven years ago.

When I fell ill, few people had heard of ME unless they knew someone who had it. Things have changed for the better, but there is still a lot of confusion, even among doctors. No one knows what causes the condition or what exactly it is. There are widely varying opinions on treatment, and the letters 'ME' can even stand for two or three different things. It has about twenty different symptoms, from muscle pain and headaches to irritable bowel syndrome and tinnitus, but the main one is fatigue. You feel tired all the time and if you do anything you feel exhausted—hence the alternative name of 'chronic fatigue syndrome', which really does not do it justice. I was so out of it to begin with that it was several months before I realized that I was not praying.

So I am left feeling ill, bored and frustrated—which in itself does not do my health any good. I have had to totally readjust my life and my attitudes. I do not give thanks for my health—be honest, who does when they have it?—but I give thanks that I am not as ill as some people and that I have my mother to look after me. I do not like being dependent but maybe that is a lesson about my relationship with God.

I have not mastered all the lessons but I am learning. I hope that writing this book will be part of the process, leading me towards wholeness if not towards physical healing. Maybe God will improve my health so that I can finish the book; maybe I will just have to learn to be more patient and to focus better. Either way, I will let you know when I get to the end.

There is one thought that has been going round in my head since I fell ill. One of the most important events of the Methodist year is the Covenant Service at the beginning of January, when we rededicate ourselves to God. It centres around the Covenant Prayer, the traditional form of which includes the words, 'Let me be employed for you or laid aside for you'. I never fancied being laid aside. I never saw how that could be part of God's plan. Then it happened. I still do not like it. I still do not understand it. I am learning to see God in it, if only mistily.

Much of what is contained in this book I have tried out for myself.

Other material has been tried by people I know who have been in different circumstances from my own. There are also bits and pieces I have picked up from here and there. I cannot guarantee that any of it will 'work' for you but I hope you will find something helpful. It is a learning process for me too, but it is in the learning that I hope I can be of most use to others who find themselves in a similar situation.

CHAPTER 2

EGYPT

Read Exodus 1—13 (or as much of it as you feel comfortable with).

The first thing we need to do if we are to get to the Promised Land is to find out where we are coming from.

It is true to say that we do not know much about the Israelites as individuals. We do not know their personal histories, only the history of the group: Joseph saves Egypt and he and his family are honoured; time passes and future Pharaohs forget the reason for the Israelites' privileged status; the Israelites are enslaved, they cry out to God, and God leads them out of Egypt. This is history on the grand scale and it is hard to see them as real people, people like us. At the beginning of the 21st century we put a premium on the individual rather than the group.

Who are we?

It would be impossible to define every individual who reads this book but people do tend to fall into one of a selection of categories—or they might be a combination of various aspects of those categories. There are people who might appear to be in the wilderness but who have actually come in to be alongside those who are genuinely in exile. These are people to be admired, but this book is not really for them.

They are dealing with other people's problems, not their own.

Another group of people who might appear to be in the wilderness really do have problems of their own but something about them helps them to cope. Perhaps it is their background or upbringing, but somehow they bounce back. However bad the situation, they can always see the light at the end of the tunnel. If that is you, then you can be a real help to the rest of us. You can show us how it is done. You may not feel you know the answers, but simply by being there you give the rest of us something to aim for.

But there are a lot of people in this world who are lonely, angry and defensive. Often they have good reason to be. Life keeps on throwing rocks at them and they build walls to protect themselves. We all need defences but if there is no door in the wall we are not just stopping other people getting in, we are stopping ourselves getting out. We are restricted and even suffocated as the walls close in on us. Is that you? If it is, I suspect that you recognize the description, at least in part. I know how uncomfortable those feelings can be. I hope that this book will help. As I said in the previous chapter, I do not have all the answers but perhaps I can help you find the key for your door.

And then there are those who do not appear to be in the wilderness. Everything looks as if it is going fine for them. (Perhaps they put a lot of effort into making it look that way.) Underneath, however, they do not like themselves. Perhaps in their childhood they were never told that they were good enough. Perhaps they were bullied at school —that is a hard thing to get over. But no matter what the situation, something always undermines their confidence and they blame themselves for everything that goes wrong. Maybe they tell themselves that they're to blame, twenty times a day. Maybe they just act like it, doing stupid things that hurt themselves and other people. They make the situation worse because of the way they feel; then they blame themselves for making things worse, and like themselves even less, and do even more stupid things. It is a vicious circle, and one that is not always obvious on the surface. However, it can be broken.

Some people manage to break the circle on their own. I admire them, but their achievement is beyond most of us. Some people manage with the help of their friends. I hope that you can find that help. But we can find all the help we need if we look for it, because we have God to rely on. You cannot get better resources than those. And remember that whatever we think of ourselves, God thinks highly of us. He made us, he saved us, he loves us. Whose opinion do you want to take, his or yours?

Seeing straight

So where do we begin? By being clear where we are starting from.

Are you one of those types of people outlined above, a combination of their characteristics, or someone else entirely? Be honest, because if you are not you will get nowhere. I can only write in general terms because I do not know you personally. You will have to tailor the ideas in this book to suit yourself—and there is no point in creating a tie-dyed kaftan if you would look better in a business suit, or vice versa. So be honest all the way down the line or there is no point in proceeding.

If you are not sure of the answers to questions, do not be afraid to take time to think. Better a thorough job that takes months than a quick botched job that looks attractive but does no good in the long run. It is understandable to want to get out of the hole you are in as quickly as possible, but there is no deadline.

And besides thinking, of course, the other thing to do is pray. God knows who we are even if we do not. After all, he created us. Ask— and be prepared to listen to the answers.

There are also secular means. Do not be afraid to read a book or take a course on popular psychology. There are a lot to choose from, and many are very helpful. I know that some Christians are wary of such things but I do not believe that they should be. God gave us the ability to study and understand ourselves. If it is OK to understand our bodies and to learn how to make them better, I do not see why there should be a problem with our minds. Mental health and hygiene are just as important: if we need help with them, we should take it. We might be surprised at what we find, or the answers might be exactly what we expected.

So the first thing to understand is who we are. The second is how we came to be in exile. I covered some of the most common reasons in Chapter One but just as every person is different, everyone's circumstances will be different. Those two factors mean that everyone's wilderness will be unique.

The way you arrived in exile might be something you keep on mulling over or something you avoid thinking about because it is too painful. Both reactions are understandable. Something major and awful has happened in your life. But neither reaction is entirely healthy. We need to be able to step back and take a detached look—which is no mean feat. We need God's perspective on the situation, so again it's necessary to pray and then to look at any source of information available to us.

You probably fall into one of two rather obvious categories: those who know what their problem is and those who do not.

If you think you know what the problem is, may I ask: are you sure? Of course, if you are unemployed or bereaved you will not be mistaken about that, but there may be contributing factors that you have not thought about. Does something in your present experience remind you of something else bad that once happened, something you have never dealt with? Do you feel guilty over something, rationally or irrationally? Have you considered that you might even be ill without knowing it?

If you do not know what the problem is, ask yourself the same questions. It may be just the sense of dissatisfaction that is sweeping the modern world but there may also be an underlying cause. Illnesses such as ME and underactive thyroid can go undetected even by doctors. If you are experiencing any physical symptoms, it is worth having a thorough check-up. Simple explanations are often the correct ones, and if the help is there, take it.

As for guilt, Christianity is often accused of inventing it. This is a load of rubbish! Christians are not meant to spend their lives feeling guilty, they are meant to do something about it.

The current attitude seems to be that guilt is a bad thing, dragging people down and sapping their energy for no good purpose. It may even make them bitter. I agree with all that. However, the accepted consequence seems to be that therefore we should just abandon guilt and deny that we have anything to be guilty about. This, it seems to me, leads to one of two reactions.

The first reaction belongs to those who are able to deny their guilt. If there is nothing to feel guilty about, it means you can do anything, no matter what the consequences are for you or others. This might make you a happier person in the short term but probably not in the long term, and the effect on society can be dire.

The second reaction is that of the people whose consciences are working too well to be able to accept the current wisdom. They cannot offload their guilt simply by denying it, so they are left with no way of getting rid of it. And then they add yet another layer of guilt for not being able to get rid of it!

How God wants us to deal with guilt is simple on paper, if not entirely easy to carry out.

- First we acknowledge what we have done wrong.
- We turn to him and ask for forgiveness.
- We do whatever we can, with his help, to put things right.
- We ask for the strength and wisdom to do better next time.
- Then we start afresh.

And we do not waste our energy on guilt that benefits neither ourselves nor anyone else.

Even if we have already tried and failed at this, it is still the only effective method.

As I have said before, the most important thing is always to be honest with ourselves, even if the honest answer is to admit we do not know. If we admit we do not have all the answers, we can start looking for them. If we think we have all the answers, we will not bother to try.

Once we have looked at how we came to be in exile, the next question we need to ask is 'Where have we come from?' That was a very simple question for the Israelites to answer. They came from Egypt, where they had originally been honoured guests but where their situation had deteriorated to the point that not only were they being used as slave labour but their children were being systematically murdered. It is the kind of scenario that still shocks when we see it on the television news. But in those days the world was rather different and it seems God was a lot more inclined to take direct action rather than asking us to do it for him. The Israelites cried out to God, he heard their cry and he answered it. Celebrations all round?

No. They started complaining before they had even got to the Red Sea. I will deal with the Israelites' attitude further in Chapter Five. The point I want to make here is that the way they talked about Egypt after they had left was entirely different from their attitude while they were still there. Their memories of sitting round pots full of meat and picking out the good bits (Exodus 16:3) sound like the situation in the time of their ancestor Joseph, not that of people who had to deal with an unendurable and ever-increasing workload.

Nostalgia is not necessarily harmless. It can poison the present. A minor example would be those people who make the sweeping judgment that the new hymns are not as good as the old ones. Fair enough, there are some awful modern hymns being sung. On the other hand, the great Charles Wesley is estimated to have written between two thousand and ten thousand hymns in his lifetime, yet even the current Methodist hymn book *Hymns and Psalms* contains only about 150 of them. Why do we not sing the rest? I guess it is because they were not very good. The best remain because they have stood the test of time.

It is the same with our memories. Although our clearest memories are often of the very worst things that happen, we tend to edit out the merely dull or downbeat. I look back on my last job, packing perfume, with affection. I got on with most people, the work was regular and my take-home pay was higher than I had ever had. I have to remind myself that the hourly rate was just over two pounds, I was no good at the work and I came home every day stinking and exhausted.

It is not that I always want to look at the down side. It is simply that if we invest the past with a rosy glow, the present can look darker than it is. What was 'Egypt' like for you? Was it full of wine and roses or were you trying to make bricks while having to gather your own straw? Do you want things to go back to the way they were or do you want to move on?

Looking across the Jordan

Looking back is not always a bad thing. If a marriage has hit a rocky patch, we want to look back to that first flush of love. But it will never be exactly the same again. What we want is that first flush, plus—ardent love combined with all the maturity and experience we can now bring to the relationship. It is like that in our relationship with God or the career we want to pursue. We need to get back on track rather than actually going backwards.

Or do you want something else entirely? Is God pushing you somewhere unexpected? It may be that you cannot go back and have to go forward. It may be that you want to go forward, because the past was not that good for you. Maybe you want to strike out in a different direction, to start drawing your own map of uncharted territory—as Abraham did when God called him (Genesis 12 onwards).

I have always written odds and ends. I have notebooks dating back to when I was twelve, full of poems and ideas. I have scraps of paper dating back almost as far as my first letters. At the back of my mind I always wanted to be a writer but I was too busy getting qualifications, looking for jobs and being active at church. It was not until I had been ill for six months that my mother spotted a course called 'Writing for Publication' which I agreed to take as a back-up, in case I had difficulty finding a job when I got well. I did not get well, but here I am writing a book—not something I could have predicted.

I have to say, however, that if God wanted to push me in this direction, I wish he had chosen a gentler way of doing it. And no, I do not believe that I am ill because God wanted me to write this book. That would not make sense.

There are probably a lot of reasons why you have found yourself in the wilderness, just as there are for me; but stop and take a look around. Now that we know there is a problem, this is an opportunity to do something about it, and perhaps about other problems in our lives. The opportunites you discover might have no bearing on the original situation, just as taking up writing is not going to make me well. But is there a change God wants you to make? Is there a change you want to make? If there is, go for it.

If the Israelites had headed back towards Egypt, what would have happened to them? No one knows, but the chances are that they would have disappeared from the pages of history. Probably they would have been massacred. And God would have chosen some other nation to show the world his purposes. As it was, Moses shepherded them on their slow and painful journey to the Promised Land. As we follow them, perhaps we can learn from their mistakes.

CHAPTER 3

THE GOLDEN CALF

Read Exodus 32.

Moses is up the mountain, talking to God. He has been gone a long time—there is an awful lot to talk about. The people back on the plain are getting restless. A whispering campaign starts up: 'Is he really coming back...?'

So a group of people get together and approach Aaron: 'You're the priest. You're the elder brother. We want a god—one we can see; one like other people have.'

So Aaron tells the people to bring him their jewellery and he will make them a god and give them a religious festival—a fun one, one that is an excuse for a party. What they have forgotten, of course, is that God—the real God—can see what they are doing. Trouble is about to descend on them like the two stone tablets that Moses throws down when he finds out what has happened.

Do you have a golden calf?

Them and us

It is easy to be patronizing towards the Israelites, to say 'How could they be so stupid?' But how many of us let something usurp at least part of the place God is supposed to occupy in our lives? And even if we do not do that, is the God we are worshipping God as he really is?

There are three theories about what the golden calf represented, though two are closely related. The first is that the Israelites wanted a new god, one other than the God of their ancestors. The second is that the statue was supposed to be the real God but a version of God that they could see and touch—a version of God that was a great deal more *normal* than the one who manifested himself in a glowing cloud. The third theory is that the calf was supposed to be a throne for God, which would not tie him down so much but would still allow the people to put God firmly where they wanted him and not the other way round. The Ark of the Covenant soon fulfilled a similar function, but that was at God's instigation, not theirs. He was still free to come and go as he saw fit.

But none of those ideas of God is good enough. None of them is God as he really is and none of them will do us any good.

Why did Aaron choose to make a calf? Perhaps because bull symbolism was so strong in Egypt. Most people know that almost every animal in Egypt represented a god, from lions down to dung beetles and centipedes. The bull, however, was particularly important. There were at least three living sacred bulls at important Egyptian temples, the most famous being the Apis bull. Most of the important gods (as well as the early Egyptian kings) were in some way associated with bulls—or with cows, as in the case of Hathor, the very popular goddess of childbirth. The bull was the symbol of strength and authority. Perhaps Aaron had been impressed by the splendour of the bull cults. Perhaps he wanted to usurp some of the authority of the Egyptians, the powerful people from whom the Israelites had just escaped.

Only he came up with a calf, didn't he? Why?

(Actually, 'young bull' is a better translation than 'calf'. How young? I am allowing myself a little leeway to err on the side of the traditional.)

Perhaps the Israelites simply did not have enough gold. Or perhaps they were not prepared to give any more. This was an expensive way to go about religious observance.

Perhaps the writer of Exodus was simply expressing his contempt—because the calf is a very weak symbol. We have all seen calves, on television if not in real life, staggering around on their spindly little legs. They cannot look after themselves; they will die without their mothers or without human intervention. What kind of god would a calf make?

About the same kind of god as anything else we care to put in the place of God.

Do you have a golden calf?

What is a golden calf?

You have probably been asked this question before in one form or another: what do you put in God's place? Let me list some of the usual answers—money, status, security, power. We would all like those, at least a little bit. Did you ever meet anyone who did not want more money, even if it was only a few pounds a week?

But those are the obvious answers, and what is obvious is easier to deal with. You may have a problem in those areas. You may have had a problem and already dealt with it. Good for you. Is there anything else?

Golden calves can be trivial or they can be things that would otherwise be good—except that we have given them too high a priority. There is not much difference between giving first place to something that ought to be 33rd and giving it to something that ought to be second.

First let's consider the trivial. Did you ever meet someone with a collection that dominated their life? It might be anything from electrical insulators to pearl buttons to 1940s' paraphernalia—an attempt to recreate the decade in its entirety. When I was young I used to say I collected collections, I had so many—postcards, badges, bookmarks and more. Most of them fizzled out naturally; some I deliberately got rid of; some still sit in boxes. Some I occasionally add to. But most of the devotion that went into those

24

collections now goes into my collection of books of television series. I gave up counting them years ago but there are probably upwards of two thousand books on two hundred series—from 'Champion the Wonder Horse' through 'The Man from UNCLE' and 'The Avengers' to 'The Bill'. There are only two things that slow down the growth of this collection: lack of space and lack of income—plus the fact that I am too mean to buy a book unless I think I am getting a good deal. At one time I had to ask myself whether the collection was coming between me and God, because I was spending an awful lot of time and attention on it. I do not think it is any longer, though it is still true that one of the first places I turn when I am angry or upset is to my books. There are few better ways of getting things out of your system than a good vicarious punch-up or car chase. The trick is to appreciate the books for what they are—a gift from God—and to turn to him first.

I must emphasize that, in pointing out the pitfalls of becoming absorbed in our hobbies, I am *not* trying to be a kill-joy. The writer Adrian Plass has a character called Mrs Flushpool in his *Sacred Diary* and its sequels, who shows up the absurdity of the attitude that anything enjoyable is sinful. She believes it is a sin for her husband to be interested in building model aeroplanes. To maintain that everything we enjoy comes from the devil is to stand things on their heads. God made the world. He made it good. He made it for us to have a good time in, but when any of the things of this world start to creep in between us and God, it means that we are not having as good a time as we were intended to have. Everybody needs a hobby, but let it stay a hobby, because there is no fun like living in God's presence.

If there is something seemingly trivial in your life that comes between you and God—maybe something that would never occur to anyone else—then I suspect that deep down you already know what it is. We will look at suggestions on how to deal with it in a moment. Before that, what about the good things, the important things in your life that could become a golden calf?

Jesus was very clear that nothing, absolutely nothing in our lives should come before God. For instance, in Matthew 10:37 he says that not even our families should—and the family is top of the list for many people. Some people might find that shocking, but if they do, I think they have the wrong end of the stick. What God wants is not for us to love anyone else less (quite the opposite), but to love him more. Indeed, the more we love God, the more we will be able to love everyone else. Do you know the song 'Magic Penny' by Malvina Reynolds?

> *Love is something if you give it away,*
> *You end up having more.*
> © LEEDS MUSIC LTD

This is exactly how humans were designed to behave.

We can put many other good things in the place of God. Getting an education or training is very worthwhile, especially if it will allow us to benefit others, whether as a doctor or an actor. But it can also become a golden calf. Good works can be put in the place of God, and the Bible warns against this (for example, Ephesians 2:8–9). We can try to save the world by our own efforts, through some plan or scheme. History shows that this does not work. Perhaps it improves things a little; perhaps it ends in disaster. Either way, we wear ourselves out for little return if we do not turn to the source of all improvements. Only God can bring in the Kingdom of God—with our help. It is amazing that he lets us help him, but we need to put him first to get the best results.

Even the Church itself can become a golden calf—your local church, your denomination or the universal Church. That discussion belongs more in the next chapter but do bear in mind the fact that the worst idolatry often happens when we take the best things and put them in the place of the Best, just as the worst sins are often a corruption of what ought to be the best in our lives. According to the old story, Lucifer was the highest of the angels—and fell to become Satan.

The practical stuff

So what do we need to do? Again, think and pray. Is there anything that is keeping you away from God—getting in the way because it has usurped his role? It is probably only a partial blockage but it needs to be cleared out if you are to be functioning properly.

How do you recognize something that is usurping God's role? Look at the Israelites. God disposed the Egyptians to shower them with gifts, particularly gold, when they left (Exodus 12:35–36). (Now that is a miracle, considering the destruction that had just happened.) Those gifts could have done a lot for the Israelites but they chose to melt the gold down and turn it into a calf. Their false 'god' meant something to them so they were prepared to give towards it.

What do you give your money to? More important, what do you give your time and attention to? If you spend more time thinking about your favourite football team than you do about God, then you have a problem. If you pay more attention to the Lottery numbers on Saturday night than you do to the sermon on Sunday morning then you definitely have a problem. Remember what Jesus says about God and Mammon (Matthew 6:24). Whom are you relying on?

Getting a sense of proportion

If you have taken a good look and cannot find anything that is coming between you and God, look again. If you take a second look and still cannot find anything, good for you. No problem affects everyone, and if you have escaped this major one, that is excellent.

If you have identified something wrong, the first thing is not to go over the top. There was a story widely reported in the press a few years ago about a lady who joined an organization which claims to be Christian but has a bad reputation. The elders told her that she loved her cat more than she loved God. Their solution was for her to have the cat put down. It is a great shame that no one pointed out to her that God loved the cat too. Why else would he have created it?

This is the sort of thing that gets Christians a bad name. It is an extreme example, although I dare say there are worse ones. The point is, do not throw the baby out with the bath water. If something is good, it is good. It will simply be better if it occupies its proper place.

One of my friends used to write letters full of how bad she was and how she was letting God down. Fortunately she has lightened up a little recently, but all along she was one of the best Christians I knew. Besides the fact that God does not want us to be miserable, just think how much more energy she would have had to do what he wanted if she had not been using up so much worrying about what she was doing wrong. Strike a balance. Take a good look at yourself but do not keep ferreting away at your shortcomings when you ought to be thinking about something different. That in itself is a form of idolatry —putting your own unworthiness first.

Once you have identified a problem, think about the best way to deal with it. A book such as this can only ever give a general view, and your problem is personal to you. Think about it and pray about it. Ask and, more importantly, listen, because God will have the answer if you are prepared to listen. Of course, like all prayers the answer may be a while in coming, and may not arrive in the form you expect. Keep your eyes and ears open.

Besides prayer, God has given us something else which is always a great help—common sense. Some people wait around for ages looking for a 'sign', when the answer they need is right under their nose. There is a joke about a man who gets caught in a flood. A Land Rover comes past and offers him a ride out of his house but he says: 'No thanks, God will save me.' The waters continue to rise and he has to go up to the next floor of his house. A boat comes past and again the people offer him a ride out of there. Again he replies: 'No thanks, God will save me.' But the flood waters keep on rising and eventually he is sitting on his roof. A helicopter comes past and again offers to rescue him but gets the same reply. The waters keep rising and rising and eventually he drowns. He gets to heaven, storms up to God's throne and demands 'Why didn't you save me? I had faith in you.' And God replies: 'I sent you a Land Rover, a boat and a helicopter. What more do you want?'

Sometimes the answer is so obvious that we miss it. Why should God go around sending signs and wonders when an item on a TV programme would work just as well? Look at the story of Naaman (2 Kings 5). He was extremely miffed that all he needed to do to be cured of leprosy was to bathe seven times in the Jordan. It was not even as impressive a river as the ones they had back home in Syria—a silly attitude, but one that we might catch ourselves in sometimes.

What does your problem need? If it is something harmful in itself—alcohol, tobacco, gambling—then take any help you can to get rid of it. There is plenty of help around these days, from the National Health Service, charities and even the BBC on regular occasions. There is no quick fix for such serious problems but there is light at the end of the tunnel.

Take a look and see if there is any way in which your problem can be turned around and used for God. It might help you fundraise, evangelize or simply help others to enjoy themselves. DIY can be done for people who cannot do-it-themselves. Skills can be taught to others. Interests can be shared. Drama or music are obvious examples —they can be used in all kinds of ways—but could you make something helpful to others out of an interest in jigsaw puzzles? What could you do with all those old magazines sitting around? God gave us our talents and interests just as much as he gave us the showier spiritual gifts, though we tend to forget that. They can all be used in his service.

Maybe it is just that you need to tone things down a little. Do not abandon your interest altogether but let the rest of life get a look in. Something that helps you to relax is good; anything that takes over your life is not.

Love for others is never a sin but we can only love them to the fullest extent when that love is filtered through God.

The most dangerous idol

Having said all that, there is one idol that is much harder to deal with—God himself. Or rather, our false perceptions of God.

Each one of us has a slightly different view of God and I think that that is a good thing. Our individual minds are too limited to see God as he really is but I believe that the insights of each person make up a mosaic that comes close to showing what God really is. By sharing our insights, we learn and grow.

But some people's ideas are just too off-beam. In fact, in some cases they are simply not true, and if they are not true they can be down-right harmful. They can put us into the wilderness rather than getting us out of it. We have all seen people spouting off on the television—people who call themselves Christians but actually preach hate and prejudice; people in whose mouths the name of God is blasphemous.

If your idea of God causes you to hate anyone on earth, then it is wrong. And when I say 'anyone', I include yourself. We should not hate 'sinners', or members of other faiths, and certainly not other Christians—and, I repeat, not yourself.

What kind of image of God causes people to react with hatred? A harsh, angry, demanding one. Sometimes this image is called the 'Old Testament God' but that is unfair. Some passages in the Old Testament *would* lead you to think that God was like that—the passage in which God commends the Levites for slaughtering those who worshipped the golden calf, for instance (Exodus 32:29). But the vast majority of the Bible shows us that this is not the whole picture. Prophets like Isaiah and Ezekiel tell us that God is slow to anger, abounding in grace and does not desire the death of a sinner (for example, Ezekiel 33:11).

Moreover, the ultimate revelation of God is Jesus, and the over-whelming quality we see in Jesus is sacrificial love. If you want a neat exposition of this in the Old Testament, try the prophet Hosea—the first of the Minor Prophets in your Bible.

It seems odd and sad to me that some people put such a gulf between God the Father and Jesus that while they can regard Jesus as kind and loving, they regard God as some kind of abusive father. They blame him for Jesus' death on the cross and cannot see that although the first and second persons of the Trinity are not identical, they are the same in character. This is a paradox that has occupied theologians for centuries. Perhaps the simplest thing to say is that the Father and Son are bound together so closely in love that nothing in creation could fit between them and that what one feels and suffers, the other does too. Therefore, if Jesus loves us enough to live and die for us, so does the whole Trinity. Jesus really is the revelation of God's love. Think of it in terms of an ordinary, close family: if one member is happy, the rest are happy; if one is in pain, the rest feel that pain.

Another common false image, perhaps more common these days, is of a remote God—someone who set the planets spinning, then retired to put his feet up. The familiar words of Psalm 8:4, 'What is man that thou art mindful of him?', taken alone, might contribute to this image. Some people think that science has pushed God out to the fringes. Some people think that he is just not interested in them personally. Surely that leaves us alone in the wilderness? Any life can seem like a wilderness if we do not think God is there for us.

In Psalm 8, 'What is man that thou art mindful of him?' is followed by 'Yet you have made him little lower than a god'—or even 'God', depending on which translation you read (v. 5). Our God is both transcendent and immanent—that is, he is both over everything and present here and now; infinite and infinitely remote on the one hand, nearer to us than the air we breathe on the other. It is interesting that many physicists these days are religious. These ideas can fit in very well with modern science, rather to many people's surprise. Gabriel gave Jesus the name Immanuel—'God with us'. The name still applies.

A third false idea is of a God with whom you can do deals or whom you have to placate. This can be a half-full or half-empty sort of dilemma: can you get something out of him or do you need to keep him happy? It can be linked with the 'angry God' image or it can creep into people's thinking by other routes.

There is a Greek legend about Hippolytas, the son of Theseus and Hippolyta. He spent all his time trying to please Artemis, goddess of hunting and celibacy. Not surprisingly, this annoyed Aphrodite, goddess of love, who had him killed—the moral of the story being 'if you believe in more than one god, you had better buy them all off equally'.

But you can see the same kind of mentality in people who believe in the one God. In the Middle Ages, some people tried to buy him off literally. The sale of indulgences was the most obvious excess, whereby people bought a certificate that said they had been let off a certain amount of their sins, but others paid for Masses to be said for their souls, others set up charities in their wills and still others built churches. Some of these people would have had pure motives but others were trying to buy themselves or their relatives out of trouble with God.

These days, this approach is likely to be more subtle and small-scale, but have you ever prayed, 'If I do this, I'd like that to happen'? Ever thought, 'If I don't do this, God will come down on me like a ton of bricks'? Some people think that anything bad that happens is an indication that they have not kept God sweet—have not paid enough into the 'goodness' bank to avoid him getting back at them.

Trying to bribe God is a sin. We can see this all through the Bible, from God's frequent complaints about Israel offering big sacrifices in order to get out of doing what is right to Jesus' condemnation of hypocrites. Buying God off can have nothing to do with material goods: it can also be done with outward piety or trading off one good deed against another (Isaiah 1:11–17; Mark 7:10–13). Bribing God is also counter-productive. If you try to bribe an honest official, is he more or less likely to do what you want? Likewise, God may withhold even good things to teach us that that is not the way to conduct ourselves.

On the other hand, God does not demand more from us than we can give. 'My yoke is easy, and my burden is light,' said Jesus (Matthew 11:30). Yes, he wants our whole lives, but only so that he can show us how to do what is best for us. He is our maker, after all, and he knows the design specifications better than anyone.

I am sure there are more false images—the idea of a wishy-washy

God, for instance. Perhaps there are as many wrong ideas about God as there are right ones. But what do we do about them?

Fixing the problem

Read the Bible and pray. I have already said that people can get the wrong impression of God from the Bible itself. That usually happens because they are overly selective. If you take a few verses out of context, you can make them mean almost anything. To understand correctly, you need to look at the passage *in situ*. Do the surrounding verses or chapters modify the meaning?

Even more importantly, take the Bible as a whole. Does your interpretation of a passage accord with what other books say? Does it accord with what Jesus said? If not, you have a problem. Look again; think again. Pray for the Holy Spirit's help. Read a good commentary. If people have taken the time to study the Bible in all its aspects, it is ridiculous for us not to avail ourselves of their assistance.

This applies to all issues in the Bible, not just our image of God. What we read into a Bible passage is not necessarily what God intends. The case of slavery is sometimes quoted. Those who defended slavery in the 19th century could quote directly from the Bible, in which keeping slaves was an acknowledged fact. Those in favour of abolition had to argue from the spirit of the Bible as a whole: if we are all made in the image of God and saved by Jesus, how can one person buy and sell another? Yet no Christian nowadays would dream of defending slavery. We have to understand the Bible as God intended us to see it and in its pages we can then see him. How did he intend us to approach it? With openness, with thoughtfulness, with study, and guided by the Spirit of love exemplified by Jesus.

I am not saying that there is only ever one correct way to interpret any passage. The Holy Spirit can interpret it to us in whatever way is appropriate to our situation. Also, the Holy Spirit's interpretation is very unlikely to arrive in a clap of thunder. It will probably just be that something feels right to us or was recommended to us by someone we trust. And the Spirit can work just as well through our minds as through our hearts.

Once more we turn to prayer. I believe that the underlying purpose of prayer is to build up our relationship with God. You cannot build up a relationship with someone without talking and listening, without spending time together. How else do you get to know what they are really like?

Talking to God is not usually a problem but it can be under some circumstances. This may be the case if you are in the desert. But however much you don't *feel* like talking to him, going with this feeling only makes the problem worse. It may even be the root cause.

Once, after I had preached on prayer at a local church, an elderly member of the congregation told me that he could not pray because he was so angry with God about the death of his wife. The only thing I could say to him was to tell God he was angry. God knows our true feelings so we might as well be honest with him. He can cope with our anger and pain and would much rather we took it out on him than on others or ourselves. Look at Job. He shouted and railed at God for ages. All his friends told him off for his behaviour, but when God finally appears at the end of the book, he doesn't rebuke Job. In fact, God justifies him (see Job 42:7–17). God can do something about the anger or the desert experience, if we let him.

Listening to God is what more people find difficult. Let's face it, if you say something, God is not going to come straight back with a voice from the sky. (At least, it is not very likely!) You might have to wait a while for an answer and it might come in a form that is not easy to spot. Generally we have to be prepared for answers at any time and in any form. We have to be open. There is no easy solution to this except constant practice and attention: the more you try it, the easier it becomes.

Some people can sit for hours simply waiting on God and enjoying his company. I have to confess, my mind tends to wander. I am better at a lot of short prayers spaced out over the day, but that approach does not really lend itself to listening. If I do want to pray for a longer time, it helps if I keep my hands occupied. That may sound odd, but it stops me drifting off on to what I saw on television last night or what I should be doing tomorrow. (Those might both be legitimate subjects for prayer but there is a time and a place for everything.) So a solitary hobby that is more physical than mental can be an aid to prayer. There are lots of other aids. You might find it helpful playing music or locking yourself in the bathroom or even sitting on the bus, surrounded by noise but nothing that need concern you. You should be able to find a variation that suits you.

But remember, God can show himself through other people, circumstances, a magazine, a sunset or a television programme— whatever he likes, and whatever is appropriate to you. If you are putting him first, if you are giving him your time and attention, you will see his answer. If you are living with a golden calf, if you are letting something else drown out the still, small voice, you could miss it. As the TV slogan goes: 'miss it, miss out'. It is only by following his voice that we can get through the wilderness.

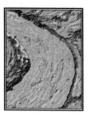

CHAPTER 4

SINFUL INCENSE

Read Leviticus 10.

The title of this chapter comes from outside Exodus but it belongs in the same line of stories. Israel is still stuck in the desert having problems. Here is one of those odd stories that litter the early part of the Bible. Aaron and his sons have just been made priests but two of the sons, Nadab and Abihu, do something they should not, and get zapped (Leviticus 10:2). It is one of those incidents that might lead us to an unfortunate image of God. (King Uzziah gets off rather more lightly for a more blatant example of the same thing in 2 Chronicles 26.) That is not the issue I want to talk about now, however.

This book is about the things that make us feel we are in the wilderness, and it is a sad fact of life that some of the biggest problems we can have can be caused by religion. Not God—religion; there is a big difference. You will not find many Christians who admit it to outsiders, but there are few of us who have not had difficulties with the church, at either a local or a wider level. Non-Christians are all too happy to admit it. It ranks right up there with the problem of evil as a reason why people do not become Christians. Apparently it was the behaviour of those who said they followed Christ that put Gandhi off becoming one of them. Even closer to our own time, many of those who arrived in Britain from the West Indies in the 1950s/60s expected to find a welcome in the Church but instead found that they were turned out. If people will even turn away good Christians for something as simple as the colour of their skin, what happens to those who are not Christians, those who have characteristics we can really object to? These incidents may have been forty years ago and more but I am not entirely convinced that things are so different today.

There are also the problems we cause ourselves through religion, which can be just as bad. (I will discuss those in more detail shortly.) All these things can push us towards the wilderness.

The human Church

First of all, we should admit that the Church is never going to be perfect. It might be inspired by the Spirit of God but it is made up of human beings. Human beings are not perfect, as I expect you have noticed. A collection of human beings can be either better or worse than an individual. With the Holy Spirit's help, the Church should be better, but rather too often it ends up seriously worse.

There are sins that beset the Church as an institution and sins that beset its individual representatives. As an institution, perhaps the most common are rigidity and exclusivity. I am aware that any large group of people needs some kind of structure: the Church could not have continued as the loose collection of free-form groups that we see in the New Testament. I happen to think that is rather a shame but it is hard to see how it could have been avoided. These days, however, I doubt the existence of any church that is not obsessed with bureaucracy, with its rules and regulations, forms and reports. I was told at one training day that ordained ministry consisted of the three Ps— preaching, pastoral work and paperwork.

To me, this is all wrong. Yes, the head office needs to know what is going on, but what a waste of the local leader's time and what a shift in priorities! It wears down those who have to administer the system and does little good to those on the receiving end. And paperwork feeds on itself, expanding as it goes. The same trend can be seen in teaching, in the health service and even in police work. The Church ought to be making a stand against this draining, unproductive burden—a desert in itself. But it may seem that all this bureaucracy comes down from the top and there is nothing that can be done about it. Rules are rules.

Can anything be done? You could try. If there is some particularly daft ordinance that is driving you up the wall, you could have a go at meeting the person who drafted it and explaining the real effect it is having. The idea may have seemed a very good one in theory, but if the person in question does not see its effects on the ground, they may never know their mistake. Even if you do not succeed—and you might—simply trying may make you feel better about yourself and give you the energy for something else.

If we cannot attempt action at that level, we can help to shift the burden off those office-holders who end up with the brunt of it. Do a little here and a little there and you can create a better feeling between people in your church.

A related problem is that people can be afraid to take on a job in the church because they think they will be expected to do it for ever or would be criticized if they gave it up. Today's Church tends to have many different offices that it is expected to fill, which do not necessarily correspond with the jobs that need doing.

All this is a problem in itself, but it is also a symptom of something else. Where did spontaneity go? The Bible tells us that God is doing a new thing (see, for example, Isaiah 43:19). We look around and think, 'He's not doing it round here.' But would we let him?

Pharisees

We tend to think of the Pharisees as the bad guys of the New Testament but that is not really fair. Most of them were good, religious people who did the will of God as they saw it. The problem was, they were not prepared to see it in any other way. Likewise, the ordinary people were expecting a Messiah who would come on a warhorse to drive out the Romans. They were not expecting, and probably did not want, any other kind.

These days, we in the Church are in the position of the Pharisees. We are the religious establishment. And it worries me greatly that if Jesus were to come preaching today, the Church would not recognize him. It might even persecute him because of all his weird religious notions and his ability to make trouble. Yet his message is what so many people are longing for. They might not understand terms like salvation but they understand freedom, rest and unconditional love. If we do not let God speak, we can push other people into the desert and ourselves, too.

Would your church let Jesus preach from the pulpit? The Church of England took a dim view of John Wesley's preaching, and he was much more restrained than Jesus. Times change; people don't.

Linked to rigidity is exclusivity. This can take many forms but perhaps the most extreme are some aspects of Calvinism. I do not want to offend anyone who is a Calvinist but if you push the doctrine of predestination to the limits, think how it comes across. If God decides whom he will save and whom he will damn, with no reference to anything else, is that justice from the judge of the world? Does that make him a God of love or a monster?

Some people will say that if God gives everyone the chance to respond to his invitation and make their own decision, that makes him less than all-powerful. I would say that if he has to take every decision himself, if he *cannot* delegate, *cannot* step back and allow someone else to make a decision, *then* he is less than all-powerful. Even if I am wrong, I would rather believe in a God who was all-loving but not all-powerful than one who was all-powerful but not all-loving. Besides, history shows that those who believe themselves to be the 'elect' do not always behave well towards people whom they do not believe to be elect.

On a lesser scale, people belonging to different denominations and traditions of the Church can behave as if they were enemies rather than brothers and sisters. Thankfully, this is receding into the past. We no longer kill each other over the 'right' way to worship. But you still hear of some hurtful actions and comments. A few years ago I heard a speaker at the Greenbelt Festival declare that there were 'no Christians in the Broad Church', by which he seemed to mean anyone not of a pentecostal/evangelical persuasion. It is the one time in my life I have felt like heckling, and I am ashamed to say that I let it go. To write off a whole section of the Church like that shows ignorance as well as a lack of charity.

Of course there are whole sections of the population that the Church is supposed to reach out to but does not—or not on a regular basis. They are the very people whom Jesus preached to—'sinners'. And the most obvious 'sinners' are often the ones who respond.

I have known local congregations who have coped with people with the most difficult and disruptive problems. There was one where a gentleman regularly shouted out during the services and usually left immediately afterwards, but the congregation treated him with grace and kindness. I know one young preacher who got his father-in-law to dress up as a tramp and wander into one of his services—and was delighted by the welcoming response of the congregation. Whole denominations, like the Salvation Army, have excellent records in this field. But the fact remains that many outsiders feel that the Church would want nothing to do with them. The Church has been far too respectable for far too long.

If something in the Church is making you feel alienated, what can I say? 'Sorry', for a start. Like many Christians, I do not have the nerve to behave differently. I would like to go out and proclaim the love of God in the highways and byways but it scares the living daylights out of me simply to do it from the pulpit—and I have trained for that. But more than that, I must tell you that a church that rejects people is not the true Church. A church like that is not getting its life from Jesus, the true Vine. And for all the moss and dead wood, there is still a heart beating of the Church that looks to God rather than itself and, in loving God, loves its neighbour, and loves you.

Can we do anything to bring this Church out of the weeds that are clogging it? Probably: one person can change the world if they are the right person at the right time doing the right thing, like Francis of

Assisi, for instance, or Jesus himself. I doubt that that person is me—but this is part of the problem. Most people doubt their own abilities and may therefore miss the opportunities that they have. If you have a vision or calling, go for it. Maybe the reason you are in the wilderness is that you are sitting on that vision or allowing petty frustrations to get in your way. Those who have been alienated by the Church could be the best people to bring others into the Church. Look at all the odd characters that Jesus picked up and what they went on to do!

Even if you do not bring your dream to fruition, it is still better to have tried. You might not change everything, but you may change something. When I was doing my O-Levels I told my brother that I was aiming for a B in one of them. He told me off. I should be aiming for an A, he said. That way, even if I missed, I might still get a B. The rest of life works the same way.

Church people

But let's look again at the Church, this time as a group of individuals rather than an institution.

There are many reasons why people in the Church can cause each other problems. Although people who call themselves Christians ought to behave better than others if they obey Jesus, that is not always the case. Sad to say, some people are just plain malicious. A church can be an awful place for gossip and worse. Little can be done about such people except avoiding them or turning them to the truth. Personally, I avoid them. I do not have the guts to do otherwise and the fact is that there is no one harder to convince than someone who thinks that they are a Christian already. Such work requires the patience and fortitude of a saint. And if you have those qualities, I do not think you should be reading my book: I should be reading yours.

But very few people are deliberately malicious. Most of the harm is down to thoughtlessness, power-seeking, insecurity and bad theology.

Can you make a realistic guess at someone's motivation for making trouble for you? It makes a difference to how you deal with it. Is there a third party whose opinion you can ask, confidentially? Things that we put down to malice, because we have been hurt, may have a totally different origin, obscured because we do not know all the facts.

Thoughtlessness

Thoughtlessness is perhaps the most common cause of trouble. Someone says something hurtful off the top of their head or without knowing your situation. They have no desire to hurt, and probably no idea that they have given you pain. Or it may be that they think they know about your situation—unemployment, divorce, or whatever—but to your ears, their ideas are totally wrong. It happens all the time. You go away and stew on what they have said. The problem gets worse without their ever knowing there is something wrong, and you take anything else they say in the worst possible light.

There are two possible solutions to this: tackle the problem or walk away.

You can confront the person with what they have done. If you do this, do it with more consideration than they have shown. You do not want to leave them feeling bad. (OK, realistically, maybe you do. But that is a sin and will only leave you in the wrong. Remember what Jesus said about loving your enemies: Matthew 5:43–48.) Explain the problem. Even if you cannot get the other person to understand, they will probably be very sorry for the unintended harm they have done.

Walking away requires less courage but just as much strength. Just let the hurtful comment go. Forget about it. Act as if it never happened. If it was not intended to do harm, don't let it do harm. Don't let it hurt you. Is that allowed? Yes. Even God has to let people be sometimes, if they will not at that moment come round—and we do not have God's strength, grace and wisdom.

How many times do we unintentionally offend God, yet he does nothing about it? So act like a child of God. It is not easy. It requires a deliberate act of will on our part, and probably a lot of God's grace. Yet if you make that act of will, it may be a great relief to you. You might harm the person who offended you by your resentful attitude but the person you are most likely to hurt is yourself—so give it up.

Power-seeking

Some people come into the Church because it offers them power over others, and some people start off with the best of intentions but find such opportunities too attractive for their own good. (I wonder if this was Nadab and Abihu's problem. Were they trying to get God to conform to their way of doing things? Or did they want to demonstrate their power as priests to the people?) We can see such power-seeking in leaders throughout church history, including, in more modern times, some of those TV evangelists who have taken a fall (and maybe some who have not). However, it is far more insidious at a local level. People might not know that they are looking for power over others. They might have some grand plan to overhaul their church or evangelize the area. It is a good plan, which ought to be carried out. But the plan—and their running of it—becomes more important than the people it affects. At that point it can cease to be God's plan.

If either of these cases—deliberate or unintentional power-seeking —is alienating you from the Church, the chances are that you are not the only one. Even if only you have suffered from it so far, it could end up harming a lot of people. So do you want to deal with it on a personal level or go for a wider solution?

It might be best simply to opt out. You know your own limits. But it might be that you should speak to the person involved. Again, they may not know the harm they are doing. They may be very grateful for another point of view. It is usually a good idea to assume that someone's motives are innocent until proven otherwise. We have all been on the other side, causing untold harm unintentionally. How would we feel if others automatically assumed the worst of us?

Maybe someone else has seen the problem and is trying to do something about it. In that case it is very easy to sigh with relief and let them get on with it but it could make the world of difference if you give them your support—whether practical or moral support. The

Bible talks about those who have the gift of encouraging others (Romans 12:8), yet it is a gift on which we seem to place a low priority.

I must stress that I am not encouraging the forming of factions. That can only be a bad thing, damaging to the Church and those involved. Everything must be done in love and with an awareness that we may be wrong, not in self-righteousness.

Of course, the fourth option is to become actively involved in church plans yourself. Speak in meetings, run for office. The exact details will depend partly on the nature of the problem with the balance of power and partly on your system of church government.

You may feel that you are too weak or untalented to do anything worthwhile. That, surprisingly enough, is a good place to start—much better than thinking you can do it all on your own. You cannot, but God can. If you are in the right, he will bless you. This does not necessarily mean that you will be successful—God gives other people too much freedom for that to be a foregone conclusion—but you will have an effect. At the very least, you can improve your relationship with God. There is a fair chance that you will find your way out of the desert.

Chapter Eight of this book is on leadership. If you are thinking along those lines for the present or future, try there for further suggestions.

Insecurity

The opposite of power-seeking is insecurity, although the former might be used to compensate for the latter. By its very nature the Church attracts a lot of insecure people, and that is as it should be. Indeed, you could say that people who are too secure are the ones with the problem, if that security comes from being stuck in a very comfortable rut. The Church is for those who know they have needs. It points to God, who can fulfil those needs. So there are many people who are gradually finding their security and some who are too messed up to find security yet. Some may not find it at all in this life.

It may be that you recognize something of yourself in this. If so, you will understand this next section with your heart as well as your head.

Some insecure people make themselves feel better by putting others down. They may attack a generalized group, such as people of other ethnic origins, or they may pick on particular individuals. Hard lines if one of the victims is you! Other insecure people lash out on an unplanned basis. Our cat, Tigerlily, was badly treated before we got her. Patience and care mean that she is now much more secure but occasionally she will take a swipe at someone for no apparent reason. People are not so very different.

The best remedy for the hurt such people (or cats) have caused you is to help them with their problem. Again, have you the patience of a saint? Not many of us have, but time and love could make a whole world of difference to both of you. Making that kind of difference to a pet, seeing it come alive, is extremely fulfilling. How much more so with a human being—and how much more difficult. Yet God's grace can make it possible. Just a kind word here and a bit of forbearance there could be the beginning of a habit that God can use.

If you cannot do anything to help, again, walk away. Try to avoid getting hurt but also avoid hurting the insecure person. Otherwise you could be contributing to a vicious circle in their life.

It can be difficult to tell the difference between malice and insecurity. We are often inclined to ascribe the worst motives to others, just as we ascribe the best motives to ourselves. It is not easy to tell what really lies behind another person's actions. I suspect that there are few people, in the Church or otherwise, who deliberately set out to hurt without being hurt themselves—and it is more Christian to look for the best in the other person's motives, no matter how much damage they do.

Bad theology

As I said earlier, the best things, when perverted, become the worst, and people do the most awful things believing it is the will of God.

Think about Job's 'comforters' for a moment. They have become proverbial for all the wrong reasons, but they set out to help. They sat on the ash heap in silence with him for a week (Job 2:13)—now that is friendship. It was only when they opened their mouths that things went wrong.

Job's friends had a fixed view of the way God worked. They thought that anyone who suffered must have done something wrong (Job 4:7). That was the normal view in those days. It was contradicted by Jesus (John 9:13) and is fairly rare these days but you do still find it. Job, on the other hand, knew he had done nothing that could have caused his suffering, and was not shy in saying so: 'Till I die, I will not deny my integrity' (27:5). His friends got more and more annoyed by this and ended up making outrageous accusations that they knew were not true: 'Is it for your piety that he rebukes you and brings charges against you? Is not your wickedness great?' (Job 22:4–5).

Like I said, you do not find so many people with that sort of view these days, although they are still around. There are variations, like those who say, 'If you haven't got a job, you aren't looking'. But what I'm really talking about is the effect of this attitude rather than the specific examples of it—the effect of someone who is so convinced that they are doing God's will that they end up doing completely the opposite. This is the kind of attitude that caused the Crusades, the religious wars and the persecution of minorities up to the present day. In the 1950s film *Night of the Hunter*, it is Robert Mitchum's evil preacher who is convinced that he has a hotline to God—and convinces many other people that he has. The heroine, played by Lilian Gish, has a much more tentative relationship with God and does not know entirely what he wants or what he is up to, but she takes in the unwanted and abandoned children—rather than killing them, as the preacher wants to.

Much lower down the scale, I remember a pastor warning his congregation to be wary of people who start, 'I'm telling you this in love…'. People who have a fixed view of the way God works are hard to deal with. I sometimes wonder if the author of Job got through to his intended audience. The problem is that they believe they are right. Of course they do: we all think our views are correct, otherwise we would believe something else. It stands to reason. I would not be writing this if I thought something else was the case. But if our views are causing real hurt—I do not mean 'offence', as correct views can often cause offence—then we are almost certainly wrong.

If you are being hurt by a person like this, you are in a difficult situation. Prayer is always a help. It can guide us in how to speak to people and it can guide us to know if we are correct in our particular case. Then, you might try reasoning with the other person or discussing a relevant passage of the Bible with them. If you are tactful, they may very well be willing to listen, and there is nothing wrong with getting an idea in 'by the back door' if that is what works. Even if they do not change their views, they may be bothered by the unexpected and unwanted consequences of those views. No Christian would want to drive another out of the Church. We all need humility, a much-misunderstood virtue.

Preachers can do more than most people to help those whose theology is causing them and others a problem. Indeed, if you follow a lectionary or set pattern of readings you may find that they are pushing you in the right direction. It can be very difficult to deal with such things from the pulpit and no one wants to be accused of bias or of abusing their authority. However, it is possible to put challenging issues in general terms without targeting any person or group. This can be particularly effective if you are preaching away from your home church. Of course, you cannot be sure people will respond, and there will always be some who think, 'My neighbour should have been here to hear that', but if you do your best, their response is between them and God. Perhaps it is best to simply preach the plain gospel to them.

If you find that many people in your church share the same harmful theology or that it is being preached from the pulpit, it may be best to find another church. Sometimes you cannot win, in which case it is better to spend your energy elsewhere than to continue banging away at a brick wall. Someone other than you may be able to help those people.

Is your hurt hurting others?

Now look again at all the situations we have discussed—problems caused by thoughtlessness, power-seeking, insecurity or bad theology —and think: are you doing that to someone else?

If you are hurt, it is easy to lash out at someone else and not realize the damage you do or to feel perfectly justified in doing it. If you are insecure, you can want to cut others down to size so that they are not so threatening. And if your Christian beliefs ever cause pain to others—especially if you do not feel the pain profoundly yourself— they almost certainly need adjustment. There are times when doing what God wants can cause problems for others. It may give those you love cause to worry about you. It may cause a rift within the church because others have not caught the vision that you have. A lot of heart-searching will be necessary. If you are not bothered by other people's pain, however, then you really have a problem.

It is hard not to be defensive if someone tells us that we have hurt them. We do not want to be the bad guy. We may over-react and make things worse. Or we may think that we have been justified in what we said or did because we ourselves have been hurt—it's funny how we never allow that excuse to others, isn't it? This is a common situation in the Bible. Everyone knows Psalm 137, that begins 'By the rivers of Babylon…'. A version even made it into the charts about 25 years ago. How many people realize that the psalm-writer ends up fantasizing about smashing the heads of Babylonian infants against the rocks? (v. 9). Nasty! And even the prophet Jeremiah talked about revenge (Jeremiah 20:12, for example).

We have to allow that we may be in the wrong. Even if we were not wrong initially, as Christians we are not allowed to take revenge— partly because it will do us no good. If someone comes to tell us we have wronged them we should value their courage for being open, and have the patience to hear them out. It is a God-given opportunity to patch up the relationship, something which is to our benefit. The Bible has a lot to say about that (see Matthew 5:23–24, for example).

Another touchy situation is if you find that you don't get on with a lot of people at church. Perhaps this is not the first church where that has happened. Has it ever occurred to you that it might be your fault? Is there anything in your behaviour that might be putting other people off? If you realize that there is, do not feel bad about it—do something about it. As I said in Chapter Two, God does not want us to feel guilty. He wants us to do better next time.

So think. Is there anything about you that puts people off? Do you snap or make disparaging comments or put down other people's initiatives? Is there somebody you can ask for an honest opinion without too much embarrassment? If you cannot think of anything wrong, do not try and invent something. Just as some people think nothing is ever their fault, others think everything is their fault. Be realistic. But if there is something, do something about it.

If you want an example, look at Zacchaeus (Luke 19:1–10). He gave away half his ill-gotten gains, then offered to pay back twice the legal requirement for anything he had stolen. He must have gone from being the most unpopular man in town to the most popular (as well as from being one of the richest to one of the poorest). And was he happy? You bet he was.

Although it may not be easy to work out what you need to do, you could be the one who ends up benefiting the most, improving your relationship not only with God and other people but also with yourself. The specific ways in which you will do this are up to you.

Assorted possibilities

Are you causing yourself problems in some other way through your beliefs or behaviour? I do not want to suggest that everything is your fault. I have come across a few 'Job's comforters' myself, who insist that if you are ill it is your fault, never mind things you could change. That is extremely annoying and out of line with the Bible. On the other hand, sometimes we unwittingly do or believe something harmful.

'Flitters' are people who go from church to church, trying them out but never settling. If you move to a new area, it is perfectly reasonable to make the rounds of the local churches, to see where you fit in. Different churches suit different people. But some people never stop doing the rounds. They flit from church to church without ever settling down. Why? Because they are looking for perfection or because they do not want to make a commitment?

If they are looking for perfection, it is no wonder they do not stop. Perfection is not to be found in this life. The Church is just a bunch of people, and people are not perfect. And as some wag once said, 'If you ever find a perfect church, don't join it. You'd only spoil it.'

It is legitimate to want perfection in a church. The thing is, you do not go looking for somewhere that is perfect. You have to work towards it as part of a congregation.

Maybe the realization of their own responsibility is what scares people who will not make a commitment. It's not that the church is not good enough for them. They do not think they are good enough for that church. Or maybe they are worried that if they settle, they will actually have to start doing some work. However it is, they might be avoiding the difficulties but they are also missing the benefits. Yes, in spite of everything I have said, there are benefits to belonging to a church! The church is intended to be good for us, or rather, we are intended to be good for each other. We are supposed to provide each other with fellowship, support and comfort. In many churches that is the reality. We are supposed to be brought closer to God by each other's words and actions and by worshipping together. And, of course, the fellowship of other Christians and the traditions of the Church are supposed to stop us from developing any way-out, harmful notions of our own. By and large, it works. Recent research shows that regular churchgoers live an average of seven years longer than people who do not attend church. Apparently it is because churchgoers have less stress. Maybe there is something in the Old Testament promises of a long life after all!

So 'flitters' should put down roots, take a few chances and start to enjoy the benefits.

Then there are those who harm themselves by believing that they are unworthy. This often manifests itself in the thought that they are not worthy to take communion, though it can be in other ways— not participating in fellowship, for instance. They deny themselves possible benefits and even possible remedies. I suspect that this is occasionally a form of inverted pride—there are people who like to think of themselves as 'the chief of sinners' because at least that makes them chief of something—but normally it is a perfectly genuine concern.

The simple answer is: read the Bible. Read the Gospels in particular. How did Jesus react to sinners? What did he have to say? Who in Jesus' parable was accepted, the self-righteous Pharisee or the self-abasing tax collector? (Luke 18:9–14).

Read Exodus. There never was a more rebellious generation, yet God gave his people chance after chance after chance. He is always offering a new start and the only sensible reaction is to take it. He has done the groundwork. Christ died for you. That makes you worthy.

Try finding something worthwhile to do and that may make you feel better. If you are already doing something worthwhile, appreciate yourself for it. And pray. That always helps, because God is waiting to tell you how much he loves you.

The opposite of unworthiness is religious pride. We all tend to have a touch of one or the other. The best description I have found is in chapter 24 of *The Screwtape Letters* by C.S. Lewis, a book that everyone should read for entertainment value if nothing else. Religious pride is natural, but it can be a problem. We have found something wonderful, something which, in a sense, sets us apart from the rest of the world. Some of us have a long family pedigree behind us of preachers and church workers, while some of us found faith for ourselves. Great! Celebrate! Our faith is a wonderful thing. But just remember that it is the gift we have been given that is special, not us. Or rather, we are no more special than anyone else. Everyone created by God is of immense and equal value simply because God loves us. We are worth more than the stars, but we are not worth more than our neighbour. If it ever gets in the way of our relationship with God, or if it ever causes us to harm someone else, our pride is a problem.

(Was it religious pride that Lucifer was suffering from in the story when he tries to take God's throne? According to Isaiah 14:12–15, he wanted the other angels to worship him for his greatness—and look what happened. The best corrupted becomes the worst.)

Lastly, something many of us tend to do is to make things both rigid and complex for ourselves. I have already mentioned church bureaucracy. We do the same thing in our own lives.

We need guidelines to stop us from causing harm. They start out simple. Then we find a situation where the guidelines do not fit. So we add another layer. Then that stops fitting. We add another layer. We can go on adding until we are totally encased. Then there are the traditions and observances that we get from others. There are other people's expectations and what we feel others expect. It can end up like a ton of concrete, despite the fact that Jesus said, 'My yoke is easy and my burden is light' (Matthew 11:30).

I do not know the answer to this one, though I am very aware of the problem. Christians are called to love God and their neighbour. That is all. How come we get into such a tangle, and still do not achieve the primary objective? Perhaps the tangle is what stops us achieving it.

Perhaps we ought to go for a kind of minimalist design in our spiritual lives—chuck out the clutter. Yet I sit here surrounded by physical clutter, knowing that I would be lost without it. I have a feeling the same would be true in my spiritual life. I have to work out what is clutter to be kept and what is just junk and dust traps to be thrown out. It takes thought and prayer and reading the Bible, as usual.

The Church can help us out of the desert by fellowship and by leading us back to God. It is not supposed to put us in the wilderness. We are not supposed to end up like Aaron's sons, getting ourselves hurt through our own religious messes. Knowing God is the best thing that can happen to us. To spend time with him is a real privilege. If I have helped you sort out one little thing, this will have been a step on my recovery. Can you pass that on, so that we can all get out of here?

CHAPTER 5

MASSAH AND MERIBAH

Read Exodus 17:1–7.

Massah and Meribah—'testing' and 'quarrelling'—sums up the Israelites' relationship with God and Moses in a nutshell.

It has been pointed out that no generation lived quite so closely with God. The pillar of cloud and fire showed his presence with them. Miracles were practically an everyday occurrence. Indeed, if you count the provision of manna, they *were* an everyday occurrence. And the Israelites behaved like spoilt brats. They started complaining as soon as there was a hint of anything going wrong and they never seemed to remember the troubles God had got them out of before.

They complained about the water, as in Exodus 17. They complained about the food. They complained about God coming too close and they complained about him staying away. Anyone would think they were on some kind of package holiday, not being rescued from slavery and genocide.

Sometimes God must feel as if he cannot win. The Bible is full of people who are never satisfied. Take the people of Jesus' own time. He tells them they are behaving like sullen kids, who say, 'We played the flute for you, and you did not dance; we sang a dirge, and you did not mourn' (Matthew 11:17). In other words, they see John the

Baptist and want someone more like Jesus; they see Jesus and want someone more like John the Baptist. Whatever they have, they want something else.

Let me get one thing straight immediately: I am not saying it is always wrong to complain. Sometimes it is very right to complain. If we see injustice in the world we should speak up, especially if someone else is on the receiving end. Organizations such as Amnesty International exist largely to complain politely to governments that they are not treating their citizens properly or are not living up to their international obligations. Few people, except members of those governments, would class that as a bad thing. We can act with them or we can act on a more local scale. So complaining can be doing God's will.

Also, we all need to have a good moan sometimes. We need to get things off our chest for our own good. Bottling things up can be very dangerous but a lot of people are prone to this. It is supposed to be part of the English character in particular—'stiff upper lip' and so on—though I am not so sure of that these days. People seem to be getting both more vocal and more outwardly emotional. Complaining is a safety valve.

To use that safety valve—and we need such things if we are in the desert—we need someone to complain *to* (complain *at* might be a better phrase). An understanding friend who will take us with a pinch of salt is ideal but not everyone has access to one of those. The other person who is ideal is God.

Just as some people love complaining to God about their terrible lot in life, others do not like to. They are shy or do not want to sound ungrateful, or they think he will be angry with them. Yet if we are angry or upset, God would rather we took it out on him than on others, and if we are just letting off steam, he knows that. Moreover, there is no point in thinking that if we do not mention to God what we are feeling, he will not find out. He did make you, after all.

The psalmist often complains to God. He says, 'My life is awful. I'm ill, sick to my soul. The wicked get away with whatever they like and are rewarded for it.' But he usually ends up saying, 'I love God anyway. He'll put everything right because that's the kind of person he is.'

Let it all out and you will feel a lot better. Let it all out and your perspective will be restored.

Mind you, that does not work for everyone. With some people, the more they complain, the more they complain. Some people are always looking for someone else to blame—perhaps an amorphous 'it' like 'the government'. You can blame most things on the government, if you try hard enough. But blaming someone else may hurt the complainant if it stops them doing something about problems they could actually solve for themselves.

Some people blame minority groups who find it hard to hit back. That can result in anything from an employee being shouted at to something like the Holocaust. Once you get on that slippery slope, the gap is smaller than it looks.

Some people blame anyone they can—suing anyone in sight the moment anything goes wrong. It is good if those with a genuine grievance manage to get redress but when prisoners in jail start suing because their newspaper is late, you know matters are getting out of hand. We do not want doctors to be afraid to work in case someone takes them to court.

Most of life operates on a smaller scale but the effects can be just as corrosive—corrosive to the complainant and corrosive to the person they are complaining at.

I am assuming you have things to complain about. Everyone does, but those stuck in the desert particularly so. But do you enjoy complaining? Are you stuck in a rut complaining?

I had a friend at college who was never happy unless she was unhappy. Her greatest joy was listing all the things wrong in her life, particularly when they referred to other people. It was a curious condition but it did not seem to harm her. I am not sure whether the same would be true of most people. I am not suggesting you are in the same state but if you are fed up or depressed, are you doing all you can to alleviate your mood or are you letting it take you over?

Of course, there are more types of negative attitude than persistent grumbling. Anger and worry also qualify. They can also be the impetus behind the complaints. After leaving Egypt, some of the Israelites seemed constantly angry, and I expect many were worried. They also expressed concern over what would happen to their children (for example, Numbers 14:3).

Worry is an attitude I particularly suffer from. I am convinced that everything that can go wrong will go wrong. Every bump in the night is a burglar. Of course, the night our car did get broken into, as it stood parked on the drive, I did not hear a thing! And oh boy, do I worry when I am preaching.

My last example shows that worrying, like complaining, can be a good thing. Preaching the gospel is about as big a responsibility as you can find, and if that does not worry you, then you have a problem. On the other hand, many people these days worry and worry and worry. Woody Allen is not an isolated case.

And how much anger there is today, with people boiling over and doing stupid things, or gnashing their teeth and keeping it all in. You only have to drive down a motorway to see it.

These days, the whole of the UK seems to spend most of its time swathed in gloom. Optimism is considered naïvety. Crime, the health service, the environment—it's all going wrong; it couldn't possibly go right! That can be true sometimes, but it is no more inaccurate to believe that everything will be all right than to believe it will all go wrong. It is no wonder that 1960s nostalgia never seems to go out of fashion. People looked forward then, in hope and confidence—and they did seem to be having a lot more fun. Pre-millennial angst was supposed to give way to post-millennial optimism, but I have seen few signs of this happening (although why a change in date should have such an effect, I really do not know).

Negative feelings have their place but for many they are running out of control. We need to learn not to say 'realism' when we mean 'pessimism'. It seems that people today are more worried than they have ever been, but with less cause than they have ever had. The per capita murder rate has had a steady downward trend since the *thirteenth century*. The same is true for most other crimes. Someone I know was wondering why people in the past did not die of diseases like cancer and heart failure. The truth is that they did not live long enough to do so. Cars are getting safer—a recent survey showed that the least safe small cars today are as safe as the best three years ago—and so, to some extent, is the standard of driving. People are aware that they should not drink and drive and are starting to become aware of the dangers of speeding. Life is so safe that many people feel the need to jump out of aeroplanes or explore subterranean caves in order to get a thrill. Bungee jumping, anyone?

What about the awful events that we see on the news? Yes, war crimes and massacres are happening right across the globe. We are horrified by them. Two hundred years ago we would probably not have been bothered, if we had heard about them in the first place. But these days people are prepared to do something about them. I was watching a documentary about the New York Police Department hostage negotiation team. A member of the team was saying that twenty years ago the hostage-taker either surrendered or they shot him. Now they are prepared to spend hours talking to him—and it works.

I could list instance after instance. Country after country is abolishing the death penalty. Medical advances mean that sick or premature children who would have died only a few years ago can now survive. Moral advances mean that women, ethnic minorities and disabled people are starting to take their rightful place in society. I do not know if the world is getting any better, but there is plenty of evidence that it is not getting worse. Many countries have the resources to make things even better, yet people waste their strength moaning when they could be pushing changes forward. If we get things in proportion, we might get something done!

What about our own lives?

This is a book for people with problems, and problems do not disappear just because we wish them away. It can feel awfully artificial to say 'Well, I'm ill but I'm not as ill as so-and-so' or, 'I'm unemployed but at least I have my health.' It seems pitifully shallow.

Yet maybe that is exactly what we ought to be doing—'counting our blessings', in the old-fashioned phrase. We should not ignore what is wrong: that can make us feel worse as the problem festers under our cheerful façade. Instead, we should truthfully acknowledge what an impact it has had on us. If the problem has only just happened or has crept up on us unnoticed, we should allow ourselves a breathing space. Then we should take our eyes off the difficulties and look to the rest of our lives.

Here is something I wrote after I had been ill for about six months:

The problem with being one of the long-term sick is that you start to define yourself in terms of your illness. 'I am ill, therefore…' becomes almost as fundamental as 'I am human, therefore…'. But whereas being human is largely positive, being ill is largely negative: 'I am ill, therefore I cannot, I am not, I will not…' whatever the next phrase may be.

This, of course, is part of the illness and needs to be broken. 'I am ill but I am still myself. I am not fundamentally different from the person I was in February.' Or am I? If I am, perhaps the change is for the better. That is not the point. The point is that I am still human. I am not the illness. I am not ME, I am me. Remember that.

This was written out of my situation but I think it could apply to many of the conditions that cause the wilderness experience. Indeed, I think it could be applied to the wilderness experience itself: 'I may be in the desert but I'm still human, still a child of God; I still have more to me than that.'

When Elijah ran off into the literal desert because Jezebel was out to get him, he complained to God: 'I'm the last faithful servant you have and now they're trying to kill me. I give up.' God displayed his earthquake, wind and fire. Then in a whisper he said: 'I will protect you. I will provide for you. And no, you're not the only one left. I have seven thousand faithful servants in Israel' (1 Kings 19:10–13, 18, paraphrased).

Elijah needed to get his facts straight and he needed to trust in God. It is easy to take the good things in our lives—including God—for granted. Do a proper audit of your life. Write it down if you need to. You might be surprised. How you do it is up to you; the more artistic might want to create a graph or chart; others could try writing columns of lists with headings like 'family', 'friends', 'possessions', 'church' and so on.

Take a look at the audit and see if there is anything you want to change that you can change. Is there even anything that you can turn to your advantage? Once you have freed your mind of grumbling, matters may become clearer. Has a bad experience given you knowledge that might be useful elsewhere in your life? Does one problem give you the solution to another?

And if *you* cannot benefit by your experience, could somebody else? It is commonly accepted that the best people to talk to young girls who might end up as single mothers are girls who are single mothers, who know what it is like to drop out of school, lose their social life and all the other consequences. People respect those who know what they are talking about. It can be extremely satisfying to help people avoid pitfalls that you yourself fell into, even if it can also be very difficult.

Having a positive attitude is not a panacea for all ills but it is surprising how it can help. Tests have shown that those with optimism and determination have better standards of health and tend to recover more easily from illness.

I have to admit that this is certainly one area where I do not live up to my own advice. I tend to see the dark side of everything or else oscillate between unrealistic optimism and equally unrealistic nerves. Practising what you preach is all very well, but sometimes you have to preach better than you practise or you would end up giving very bad advice.

So how do you achieve a positive attitude? Make yourself look at the bright side of every situation. Jump on negative thoughts. Rather, jump on unhelpful thoughts. If something is bad, say so—and then do what you can to change it. If something is beyond your power to change or does not need changing, concentrate on what is good about it. Do not say, 'I'll never get this book finished and it won't be good enough anyway.' Say, 'Someone wants me to write a book'—or whatever the equivalent is in your situation.

And last but by no means least: trust God. Part of Elijah's problem was that he was relying on himself, not God. And this despite the fact that God had just conclusively proved that he and not Baal was the God of Israel—a very funny story with a shocking conclusion (1 Kings 18:16–40). So if one of the most famous prophets can behave like that, it is no great surprise that we often leave God out of the equation.

Real faith is like that of Shadrach, Meshach and Abednego when they were about to be thrown into the furnace for worshipping God and not the king's statue (Daniel 3). They said, 'We believe God will save us. And even if he doesn't, we will still worship him.' That is what Christians aspire to, though it is impossible to say how many would live up to that standard if they were put to the test. A lot more people ignore God when things are going well and blame him when they are not.

It might seem like an odd way to behave, believing in God in spite of circumstances, yet it is curiously fulfilling. Believing in God when we get something out of him is easy but empty. Believing in someone when times are hard is the test of a real relationship and we are meant to be in relationships. Most particularly, we are meant to be in a relationship with God. We have to work on that relationship just as we would on a relationship with a human being.

Since we are not necessarily good at this, sometimes God needs to give us a shock in order to get through to us. Thankfully, it is no longer widely believed that all suffering is simply God's way of teaching us something. That view is in some ways worse than believing that people suffer because they have sinned. At least the latter has some sense of justice, if not mercy. The former makes God into a cruel schoolmaster. We should not throw the baby out with the bath water, however. Just as some people do suffer because of the wrong they have done (like getting sent to jail if you have committed a crime), God sometimes—reluctantly and when all else fails—uses a bad experience to show us what we need to see. How many people have learnt to follow their dream only after being made unemployed? Or turned their lives around after nearly killing themselves with drink or drugs? And God can use the wrong that others have done to us to show us the good that we can do. Everyone admires people like Jayne Zito and Diana Lamplugh, who have both had loved ones murdered and set out to stop it happening to others—one through campaigning on mental health issues, the other through developing awareness of personal safety. I do know that God was not responsible for the murders that hit their families—human sin was—but to take our pain and turn it to good ends is a very Christian thing to do. In a way, is that not what God was doing in the crucifixion? And with God's help we can do it too.

I doubt that most people can go that far. God only expects us to do what we can. And what do we expect of him?

The theoretical knowledge that all good things come from God and that he suffers with us in our pain is not enough (Romans 8:28; Hebrews 2:10–18), because we are half 'head' and half 'heart'. We need to *trust* him. We need to recognize what he has done for us. We need to recognize what he is doing for us. We need to allow him in to do more.

The phrase 'let go and let God' is not exactly accurate. We need to do our bit as well, even if it is only opening up to the possibilities. Being with God makes things better, even if on the outside nothing improves. Being happy, as psychologists recognize, has very little to do with what is going on outside and everything to do with what is going on inside. Let God in there and even if you cannot see him outside—which you will probably start to do—life will start to seem a whole lot better.

Pray. Read the Bible. Open up.

If the Israelites had stopped complaining and trusted God, they would have been through the desert in no time, enjoying their land of milk and honey—a much more attractive prospect than forty years in the middle of nowhere.

CHAPTER 6

GOING ROUND IN CIRCLES

Read Numbers 14.

Going round in circles is something the Israelites must have known all about—they were doing it for forty years. They made it to Canaan in reasonably quick time, messed things up totally and spent the rest of their lives going nowhere in particular. I guess that is how many people today feel. And what about Moses? He must have got a terrible sense of déjà vu every time the Israelites started complaining. Been there, done that, worked the miracle.

Life in the desert

With the best will in the world, sometimes life does not seem to be going anywhere. We are stuck in a rut—or the world is. Everything is dull and samey but we feel sure that life is not meant to be like that. Quite true, it is not.

There is a verse of a hymn, much beloved of head teachers, that goes: 'The trivial round, the common task, Should furnish all I ought to ask' (John Keble, 1792–1866).

I hate that. I refuse to sing it. It is a terrible perversion. Life with

God, which is essentially what Christianity is, should be the most exciting thing in the world. It may not send us to the far-flung reaches of the globe or make us famous evangelists or performers—it may not or it may—but the one thing it should never be is dull. How can life with the Infinite be dull?

There are two different but linked problems here—purposelessness and boredom. Someone in the desert may well have either or both of these problems. Either can be caused by a variety of circumstances and the possible solutions may hinge on those circumstances.

The main distinction is between not knowing and not being able. Can you see no point in what you are doing? Do you have no idea how to give your activity a point? Or do you know exactly what you are supposed to be doing but something is stopping you from doing it?

The first thing is to acknowledge that some activity can be pointless. It may even get in the way of actually *doing* anything. Lots of people today work long hours, travel backwards and forwards, socialize frantically and so on. It is driving them mad and many of them know it, but they do not see how to get off the hamster wheel. It is by no means an easy feat.

I know that many people do not even have time to analyse what they are doing, so my advice is to begin with the most important thing—prayer. You can start in two seconds and work up.

'Help.'

'Help, Lord.'

'Help, Lord, I'm drowning.'

Then start adding in your personal requests. A request for a clear head might be a start. I find a good place to pray is on the bus or in the toilet. We may not use one but we all use the other. If you smoke, use that cigarette break. Everyone has some little moment when they can sneak in a prayer.

Ask God for the peace and joy he promises but also ask him about your priorities. If you are the sort of person that works well with visual information you could try drawing a chart. It does not have to be neat; it is only between you and him. Draw two overlapping circles. One is for things that have to be done, the other for the things you want to do. Try to fit the whole of your life—or your immediate problem—into one of the three compartments. Take your time. Then put it away for a little while.

Come back later and take another look. Is it accurate? Are those things what you want? And those things you do not want, do you really have to do them?

People are people, not robots

First of all, forget about what other people think. If 'other people' means your spouse, your family or true friends, they do have a claim on your life. But if 'other people' means the amorphous mass of society in general, forget them. If you are feeling miserable because of something you think they expect of you, it may well be making them miserable too but they do not have the nerve or the initiative to do anything about it. All kinds of social conventions can work that way, right down to dressing the way that is expected of you. (I hate tights! They are so uncomfortable.)

God made us all different. Was this some kind of mistake—poor quality control? No. He intended us to be different. We, however, seem to be most interested in trying to be exactly like everyone else, whether it's the clothes we wear or the virtues we endorse. We live down to the standards of the world rather than up to the image of God in us.

Does this mean we can all be rampant individualists and not give a hoot about anyone else? Of course not. We are meant to live in a community of love, each helping the other, but we can only fully be a member of that community when we are fully ourselves.

Trying to fit in may seem particularly important when we are in the wilderness. We have so many problems, we do not want to cause ourselves more. Standing out from the crowd might have helped to put us in the desert. On the other hand, denying our true identity and opinions can do the same. It was only Caleb and Joshua, who tried to persuade the Israelites to cross into the Promised Land, who were not condemned to die in the desert.

So take a long, hard look at anything you are doing simply because other people expect it of you. If it is people you love who expect these things, are you sure you are right about what they want? And if you are, do they know what it is costing you? Talk to them. They are not infallible. But if they love you, they will want the best for you. Only God combines infallibility and wanting the best.

Work

Then there are things that have to be done in order to live. Work would be the main one for most people. Fortunately, a lot of people enjoy their jobs. (Ecclesiastes stresses how important this is, especially chapter 3.) Unfortunately, many more do not.

This is difficult. Few people can afford to give up work and many do not feel they can risk changing jobs. If you have dependants, it is particularly hard. Yet work dominates the lives of so many people and it often seems that things are getting worse, despite all the new legislation such as that designed to limit working hours.

There are three possible courses of action but they need to be thought and prayed through thoroughly.

Firstly, can you make the big change? Leave work? Change career? Start your own business? None of these are to be done lightly, especially if other people are relying on us. However, even if they are, it may be the right move. Most kids would rather see their parents happy than rich. Most kids would rather see their parents, full stop. And most kids can have a sensible discussion if asked. Yesterday I read an article about a British actor working in America. He had been worried about his daughters because he did not see much of them, so he asked them if they wanted him to change his job. But because they were very keen on the TV series in which he appeared, they did not want him to. I suspect it was also because he was happy in his work and they wanted him to stay that way.

But the big change may not be necessary or possible. Ask yourself what it is that is making you unhappy. Are there one or two specific things that you can do something about? Would other people support you if you tried? Will your boss listen to reason? Instead of saying things behind his or her back, it might be worth saying them face to face (politely!) especially if you can convince the boss that your proposals would be good for the company. Happy workers are more productive, although a lot of firms seem to have a problem grasping that.

Thirdly, what if you cannot make a change? You cannot afford to move jobs even if you can find one to go to. Your boss will not listen to reason or is tied by company policy. What can you do then? The only thing left to change is yourself. That is the biggest change of all. How do you keep the problem in its rightful place, and stop it souring everything else? But that properly comes into the second half of this chapter.

Bored and frustrated

There are all kinds of things that can weigh us down. Housework—does the place really need to be spotless? Church work—is it getting in the way of doing God's will?

The point is, if we cannot see that something is doing good, we ought to take a good look as to whether we should be doing it at all. We need to make space in our lives.

Then there are things we are unable to do—or perhaps that should be 'people who are unable to do things'. This I can speak about from my own experience.

The worst thing about having ME is not so much the symptoms (though they are unpleasant) as the frustration—all the things I cannot do. These are not so much specific activities—though I do not consider myself safe to drive any longer because of a lack of concentration and the speed with which I get tired—as the fact that I can only do a little of anything. I cannot walk very far. I cannot type for long. Some days I find it hard even to read. And there are many people worse off than I am.

Some days I deliberately do things that I know are too much for me because I cannot live with not doing anything. Sometimes I need to achieve something. Sometimes I just need to have fun. My symptoms flare up afterwards but it is better than dying of boredom.

I know this is a common situation for people with ME and I guess it is similar to most long-term illnesses. In a curious way it also resembles being unemployed. That has its own frustrations—not being able to find a job, obviously, but I can remember being unable to get to places because I did not have the bus fare. I had to save up to go to the cinema and that was about the most expensive luxury I could afford. And if you do not have the bus fare, you cannot get to the job centre. If you cannot get to the job centre, you cannot see what is on offer. If you cannot see what is on offer, you cannot find a job. It's a very vicious circle.

There are lots of frustrating situations in the world, from simply being short of cash to being in prison. You might be stuck at home with children or caring for someone who is sick. It gets you down. It affects your health. It affects your relationships. It affects how you see yourself.

Some people seem to have endless patience in these situations. That can be frustrating in itself, if we feel we do not measure up to them. We have to let go of that attitude, natural though it is, and take these people as an example, not a reproach. How do they do it? I am guessing here because I am not one of those patient people—but is it because they concentrate on what they can do and not what they cannot? I am all in favour of big dreams but if we are to achieve them we have to be prepared to set about them in a realistic way. According to research, this is something that men are better at than women. They avoid what they are not good at, so that they look better. Do women not choose to do that, or do they find that circumstances do not allow it?

There must be something in your life that is worthwhile, a success, that makes you feel good. If not yet, then there can be.

Since I fell ill, I have taken up embroidery. At a basic level, you do not need to be particularly artistic (which I am not) or good with your hands (which I am not), but you can end up with something that looks like a work of art. I am particularly proud of a large and very elaborate sampler that took me three years. I learnt half-a-dozen new techniques and it looks wonderful. With the number of people now taking up the hobby, it could do something for my social life if I felt so inclined. I could join a class or a sewing circle, or acquire a pen-friend from one of the sewing magazines. It is not exactly earth-shaking but I find it very satisfying. Now I hope to learn more techniques and do my own designs. (A tip: big embroidery kits are much better value than smaller ones.)

What do you do that is satisfying, however small? There needs to be something. Get a hobby if you have not got one.

The best activities benefit someone else as well. This is not entirely altruistic. For one thing, it is true that people feel better when they have done someone a good turn. It is also true that we need to feel we have an influence on people's lives. To have no influence at all is not to exist.

In fact, it is almost impossible to have no influence on other people without being on the proverbial desert island. Everything we do interacts with the world. Even our inaction makes a difference. The thing is that we often do not see the consequences of our behaviour, for good or ill. We need to see that we have done good, however small. You can bake cakes for a bring-and-buy sale or politely pester your MP—there are dozens of charities more than happy to supply information on what to pester them about. Do not sit there and think you will never make a difference: you do not know the good that you can do. I bet Bob Geldof was surprised by the impact of Live Aid…

Getting the good times

Sometimes we just need to have fun.

Some people think that Christians are kill-joys. Some Christians do live as if they are. In the past, some sects forbade dancing or even Christmas. That, however, is not what God wants. The Bible talks far more about this life than what happens after death and it is quite clear that this life is supposed to be a good life. (Look at the descrip-tion of the Promised Land in Numbers 13, immediately before this chapter's theme passage.) That is partly because we are living it with God, but he has also set up a lot of peripheral good for us to enjoy. He created a good world and, what is more, gave us the power to be creative. There are a lot of fun things out there that are meant for us —from rainbows to chocolate to the ability to paint.

There is no need to feel guilty about having fun. Yes, there are times when we should be doing something else, just as there are things we should not do. Will your fun harm anyone else, either through action or inaction? Will it harm you? If the answer to both of these questions is a truthful 'No', then go ahead and enjoy yourself.

Access can be a problem. Most activities take time, money or effort which we may not be able to spare. This is not easily solved, but look for ways to get round the obstacle. Ask about discounts. Ask for help if you need it. Use your imagination to find an alternative or try something new. Club together with your friends.

If you really cannot do something, forget it and move on to something else. This applies to jobs, to relationships, and to most of life. We have to realize that some things are just not attainable. It's sad but true. And if we persist in running after those things, we may end up missing out on other things which may perhaps be better for us or may be more fun.

Make the best of what you have. That may sound trite, but think about it this way. Every afternoon I need to take a rest but I rarely sleep. Often I get upstairs to find the cat slap-bang in the middle of my bed so that I end up right on the edge. Which is better for me: to lie there thinking, 'I feel grotty. I wish the little rat would move,' or to relax and stroke the cat and think, 'This is nice'? (Guess which I do in real life.)

Talking of cats, pets are a whole subject in themselves. They can be very good for you. There is nothing more relaxing than hearing a cat's purr, and to win their affection is a wonderful thing. Each animal is an individual—and that does not just apply to the larger mammals. One of my sister's friends breeds hamsters, which you would think are pretty much alike, but apparently they all have their own characters. Relationships with pets develop over time but are much more simple than those with humans because of their simpler emotions and circumstances.

There can be a sense of achievement here, too. Our cat, Tigerlily, was rescued by the Cats Protection League after she had been mistreated. When we got her, she was tiny and terrified. The delight of watching her grow in size and in confidence has been indescribable. Now she behaves just like any normal cat, full of annoying habits like pushing me off the sofa when she wants to go to sleep, and we would not have it any other way. It has taken a lot of time and effort from Mum and myself but her happiness is something we can enjoy all the more because we know how much we have contributed to it.

There is a downside. It is very distressing when something bad happens to a pet. You feel that everything is your responsibility and you cannot explain to the animal what is going on. Sometimes you know something they do not. We recently discovered that Tigerlily has feline AIDS. She may live healthily for a long time, but it will get her in the end. We cried our eyes out when we were given the news but there is no way we would rewrite the last four years without her.

Even without such considerations, pets can be very costly in time and money. Taking on a pet is a big decision. You need to weigh up the consequences for you and for them. Nevertheless, they can add purpose to a purposeless life and joy to a joyless one. They are not likely to get you out of the wilderness on their own but they can certainly pull you in the right direction.

Loneliness

Perhaps this is the place to tackle loneliness, a very difficult subject.

Loneliness falls into two basic types. There is the type caused by isolation from people when you want company. That is more common for extroverts—people persons. Then there is the type more common to introverts (those more happy with their own company or with a deep connection to a few)—feeling lonely no matter how many people are around. More people may make this kind of loneliness even worse.

The first type is a lot easier to deal with than the second, though it can be a big enough problem. There are lots of places to meet people. Try something that centres on your interests, such as an adult education class. Most education centres have plenty of discounts for various groups.

If, for whatever reason, you cannot get out, perhaps you could set something up at your own home, such as a self-help group for whatever your particular problem is or, again, something to do with your hobbies such as a sewing circle or writers' group.

If you cannot manage face-to-face contact for some reason, there are always penfriends. Writing to people might not be so satisfying but it is better than nothing. Many special interest magazines, societies and fan clubs have a penpals column. Certain charities set up penfriends for people in difficult circumstances, such as death row prisoners in America. This can be rewarding but also emotionally draining, and is not to be taken on lightly.

These days we also have the Internet. This kind of contact can operate on a superficial level, without commitment, which may be what you want. On the other hand, everyone has heard stories of couples who have met and married through it. Personally, I have joined a writers' group online.

It may take an effort to cultivate contact like this, especially if you are used to friendship just happening. However, if you are an extrovert you need that contact for your emotional survival. Even if you want to cut yourself off, this is not a good idea. If nothing else, think how much you may be able to give to others through your friendship. You may be helping them out of their desert.

Lonely in a crowd

The second type of loneliness is much more difficult to do anything about. This is the type I have always had a problem with. Every time I went to a new school or college, my mother told me that I would meet people like me. I did not, though I usually made a few friends. It was not until I took my second crack at getting a degree that I did meet a few kindred spirits. Then came another gap, until I joined my writers' group. That does not add up to many people but I have survived and occasionally even prospered.

I have by no means solved the problem but here are a few recommendations based on personal experience.

Try any of the tactics recommended for extroverts and, while you're at it, brush up on your social skills. This tends to be something introverts are rather lacking in. It might not provide the deep contact you are probably looking for—or it might, you never know—but at least it should make the time pass more pleasantly.

Hold on to the friends (and family) you have. There are times when it is necessary to let people go but it is always a shame to let a friendship slip away for lack of effort.

Turn to God. Yes, of course, everyone should turn to God but different people are better at keeping different commandments. Jesus told us to love God with all our heart, soul, mind and strength, and to love our neighbour as ourselves (Mark 12:28–34), but some people are better at the former and some at the latter. Would a contemplative lifestyle, or a version of it, suit you? In other words, although we all need human contact, that big gap in your life might actually need to be filled by keeping company with God.

This last suggestion might sound defeatist but I do not intend it to be: try living in a fantasy world. Maybe that is putting it a bit strongly, but try filling the gap creatively. There is nothing wrong with using your imagination so long as you can tell where the boundary between fantasy and reality is. You could just be daydreaming to relieve stress or you could be on your way to a career as a writer. At the very least you can have a lot of fun, and you might find that the loneliness is not so important any more. (But do remember to dip back into reality every now and then!)

Pulling the strands together

This chapter seems to have covered a lot more than simply 'going round in circles' but that is because a sense of pointlessness and purposelessness feeds into all the other things discussed. It is something that hits everyone now and again and it seems particularly common in our age; you might say it was the whole point of this book. But such feelings can be overcome. If you can, follow your dream. Weigh the price carefully but be prepared to take a risk. And if you do not have a dream, get one. No one gets anywhere without one.

Use your time in the wilderness to take stock and listen out for any messages, however unlikely, that God might be sending you. No one is supposed to be stuck in a rut. With his help you can get out of it.

CHAPTER 7

THE SABBATH

Read Exodus 20:8–11.

In this leisure-based world, it is not often remembered that the weekend was invented by the Israelites—or maybe that should be God. He was the first person to take Saturday off at the beginning of Genesis.

The words 'Sabbath' and 'weekend' conjure up very different ideas but I am not sure that they should. The latter is just a secular, two-day version of the former. All the good bits were written in by God. But for once the secular world seems to have more idea of what it is for.

Thou Shalt Not...

The Israelites' Sabbath was Saturday, but Sunday has taken its place for Christians, as a weekly reminder of *Easter* Sunday. I think Christians have got Sunday tied up in two different knots, a traditional one and a modern one. The world seems more aware of the traditional problem, which involves one of those 'thou shalt nots' that Christians seem to get tarred with—a rule to stop you doing something rather than a liberating experience. 'Thou shalt not do anything—anything at all except go to church—on Sunday.' This is not exactly what the Bible says. The Bible says you should not *work* on a Sunday. There's a big difference. Take the day off!

To be honest, we have no idea what the Israelites did on the Sabbath. They worshipped God, I am sure, but what else? I do not know. Went visiting, perhaps? Had a sing-song? I would like to imagine Moses putting his feet up, not having to deal with anyone else's problems for a change. I bet his wife Zipporah was glad of it as the only day she got to see him.

Perhaps that sounds a little lax. We know that the Israelites did take the issue very seriously. Sabbath breakers were stoned (Numbers 15:32–36). This is not something that commends itself to modern Christians but we have to remember that the principle was important enough to make its way into the Ten Commandments (Exodus 20:8–11; Deuteronomy 5:12–15).

We might ask the question, 'Why should God need a rest?' I presume he was setting us an example. We run around like nobody's business but God knows that we need time off, to relax. Sunday is not a day to feel that we have to sit immobile in our chairs if we are not in church (or even if we are in church). Sunday is for enjoying ourselves. I first started thinking about this when I was taking a Judaism course as part of the religious studies component of my degree. The word most associated with the Sabbath in Judaism is 'delight' and the rituals are designed to enhance that delight. I think we have a lot to learn in that respect.

As Jesus said, the Sabbath was made for man and not man for the Sabbath (Mark 2:27). It is for our rest and recreation. We do have to remember one thing, however: we must not be selfish in our enjoyment of it. The commandment was a reminder that the Israelites had had no choice about time off when they were slaves in Egypt. They were not their own people, they simply had to do as they were told. The Sabbath was designed not just for masters but also for servants—for everybody. Your wife got the day off, your kids got the day off, your workers got the day off and even your animals got the day off. Everybody needed it, everybody got it.

Most people these days do not have domestic servants (although whoever cooks Sunday lunch might not feel that way). However, much leisure activity these days means that other people have to work. Closing businesses on Sundays is not so much about getting people to go to church—that is an entirely separate matter—as about making sure they are not being exploited. The Old Testament prophets got very hot under the collar about exploitation of workers (see Isaiah 58:3). Supposedly, protection is written into the law for those who do not want to work on Sundays. But if you do not sign the contract, you do not get the job; and if you refuse a job, you endanger your unemployment benefit. This is a social justice issue, and Christ-ians ought to be in the forefront of social justice.

A detailed discussion of Sunday trading is outside the scope of this book—though we should remember that these kinds of pressures could be putting others into the desert. Surely we of all people want to avoid that. The question here is, what is the Sabbath doing for you? Is it renewing your strength or wearing you down?

I have dealt with the traditional problem briefly as my guess is that it affects few people nowadays. I am about the last person I know who was frowned on for doing school homework on Sundays. Nor were we allowed to buy ice-cream. (As you might guess, I agree with the former and disagree with the latter, though still remembering the proviso about how buying ice-cream might be spoiling someone else's Sabbath.) Most Christians have taken to heart what Jesus said about the Sabbath being made for man. They have certainly taken to heart what he said about doing good on the Sabbath (Mark 3:4). In fact, they might be doing a little too much good.

Going to the opposite extreme

Let's face it, for many Christians Sunday is the busiest day of the week.

I am a lay preacher. Until quite recently, I was also a church steward—one of the lay people responsible for the practical running of the church. At one point I was also working as a volunteer on the local radio station's religious programmes. Sunday was a case of running here, there and everywhere—all on God's business, so all perfectly legitimate for Sunday.

What a hassle—not exactly a day of rest, and not exactly unusual, I'll bet. Many Christians are so busy doing God's work on the Sabbath that they do not have time to remember what he said about the Sabbath. Some of them barely have time to remember God.

What about Jesus? He challenged the religious conventions of the day by healing people (Matthew 12:9–14) on the Sabbath, when the religious authorities said that no work should be done. What does that really say about what we should be doing?

For a start, let us look at how things actually stood in Jesus' day. The rules did not say that you could not do good on that day. If someone was ill you could stop them getting any worse, for instance. You could deal with life-threatening situations. What Jesus did, however, was to demonstrate that God did not want anyone to suffer any longer than was completely necessary. He effected total cures, rather than just maintaining the status quo. (Jesus was never very good with the status quo!)

But (and it is a big but) every time this happened (for example, Luke 13:10–17), he was responding to an immediate need. Someone was in trouble and it could not wait. What he did not do was to sit down and go through the paperwork. Everyday tasks were for every day, not for the Lord's Day, whether they were God's work or not. If someone was hungry or in pain, that was immediate. Very little else was. But we are locked into an organizational structure that may or may not collapse without our contribution. Preachers have to preach on Sundays because that is when the services are held. Likewise stewards have to do their stewarding. And there are often too many jobs and too few people—so does Sunday always have to be a day of no rest?

Again, I do not have all the answers to this question. Many people would really like to give up some of their church jobs but feel obliged to keep on for fear of dumping things on someone else. Or maybe there *is* no one else to do the work. Some of the most efficiently run churches I know are those effectively run by one person or one family.

There are a few things that can be done. Get rid of everything on a Sunday that you do not have to, or do not want to, do. If it is your pride and joy to produce a Sunday lunch consisting of a roast and all the trimmings every week, great. I hope everyone appreciates it. But if it is something you feel obliged to do, try changing it in some way. Pick up tips from books or magazines. Try missing out some elements. Try not cooking on Sunday at all. (Another idea I picked up from my Judaism class is the usefulness of a slow cooker. It can be set up the night before, leaving your morning free. Would your family really mind?)

Are there any traditions in your family that are kept up for the sake of it but whose only meaning now is more work or more restrictions? Talk it over and if everyone else feels the same way, dump the traditions.

And what about church work? It is important not to let people down, but if you are too worn out to be giving of your best, that is not good for you or anyone else. The apostle Paul might have been able to be all things to all men (1 Corinthians 9:19–22) but most of us cannot manage it. It doesn't sound as if it did Paul's health much good, either (2 Corinthians 12:7).

What are you best at? What is the most important thing you can do for your church? The answers to those two questions are not necessarily the same but they are probably related. And when is the best time to do your particular job? It might be Sunday, but there is a good chance it is not.

Remember that you will probably be doing more people more good by doing one thing really well, than by doing a bit of this and a bit of that to try to keep everything going. Remember also that you will get far more sense of achievement out of one thing well done. That is a real boost. Wilderness people tend to suffer from low self-esteem after a while, even if that is not what put them in the desert in the first place. Something well done, a success that can be repeated, and especially one that benefits others, can be the start of the road out of there.

All this would be much easier with the help of others, but they might be waiting for you to help them. They might have exactly the same problem but not have the initiative to do anything about it. So if you have a good idea, share it. If you know something that would help you, would it help others also? You can radically reorganize your church's Sunday if that is what is best for you all. (And if it is best for the church members it will probably be God's will.)

You can begin where you like, with big ideas or small. Would it be helpful to make the service time earlier, so that people get more of the day to themselves? Or later, so that they can have a lie-in? You might not get agreement but you can bring up any ideas you like, so long as you do not try to force them on anyone. (And do remember the special problems of the church leaders. Their Sunday is worse than anyone's!)

The solutions may take generosity all round but there is supposed to be generosity in the church. In fact, you may find more under the surface than you suspected. Most people are happy to help out, provided they do not think they are going to get lumbered with something they cannot handle.

Some jobs cannot be avoided—mostly the ordinary, basic things like putting the chairs out or making sure the heating comes on early enough. Handle those as efficiently as possible rather than wasting time grumbling about them. Not grumbling is not easy but it can be as habit-forming as grumbling is—and it saves a lot of energy.

And what about the positive things?

Worship

Sunday is the main day for worship. Worship should never be boxed off from the rest of life but it is good to concentrate on it on special occasions. One day a week is fine for general purposes, though longer episodes and one-off events are excellent refreshers. And worship should be refreshing and exhilarating. I am not saying you should come out of every service bouncing up and down. It is perfectly appropriate to be thoughtful or even sombre. We do have a lot of serious things to think about, after all. What should not happen is that we come out bored, depressed or thinking, 'So what?'

Are you getting anything out of worship? Obviously your reaction is going to vary from week to week. That depends partly on your immediate circumstances and partly on the quality of the service. Even in churches where you have the same preacher or worship leader every week, some days they will be particularly inspired and some days they just will not. Any preacher will know what I am talking about. Also, not every message will speak to every member of the congregation. It can't be done: people are too diverse.

So, on average, what are you getting out of worship? If the answer is 'not much', there are several possible reasons.

It could just be a feature of your being in the wilderness. If you get everything else back together, worship will fall into place. If that is the case, keep plugging away. God has a high regard for faithfulness, whether it be in the grand gestures or (more likely) in the everyday things like turning up at church when it is raining and you have had to walk.

The second possibility is that you are at the wrong church. It may be a very godly, friendly place but churches are supposed to provide more than fellowship. If *you* are not getting spiritual food, development, call it what you will—if you are not getting something of God that you can respond to through that church—you should think about going somewhere else. That is not a decision to be taken lightly and you cannot be too picky—nowhere is going to be perfect. But it may be that another church out there is waiting for your help.

And the last suggestion is that you get out what you put in, near enough. Are you throwing yourself into worship or are you content to sit back and let someone else do it all for you? I am not talking about making a lot of noise, I am talking about what your heart and mind are doing—what your intentions are.

Some people have never learnt how to let themselves go. Some people are afraid to let go in case God actually does something with them. Frightening stuff, that. On the other hand, some people are very keen to let go and have a good time but that is all they are interested in.

Striking a balance is the best bet—being enthusiastic but not leaving your brain at the door, and always, above all, being open. We can meet God anywhere but we are supposed to meet him in worship. And if we do, there is no knowing what he will have to say.

You can combine possibilities two and three by doing something about worship at your church. Different denominations offer different opportunities for this, but these days most will welcome any new blood (or old blood, for that matter). Your own natural talents will, of course, help to define your contribution. We tend to forget that natural talents are just as much a gift of God as anything else. But do not just stick to what you have done; think of what you might do.

It might sound as if I am contradicting most of what I said about off-loading things you do on Sundays. But it is not so much about not doing anything as not doing *chores*. Besides, you might be making someone else's Sunday easier.

Worship is supposed to be the centre of our Sabbath. Actually, it is supposed to be the centre of our lives, though not necessarily in the conventional sense of going to church. It combines basking in God's love and getting ourselves ready to go out and do something. We offload all our sin and guilt; we take a good look at God and so become more like him; we pick up the gifts he is waiting to give us so that we can take care of ourselves and others—be they spiritual gifts, teaching or whatever. At least, that it is the theory. If we come away with a considerable amount of one and a bit of the other two, we are probably doing pretty well by most people's standards. And these are all things that we can do any day of the week, without going near a church, and either in company or on our own. Some people forget that. Other people forget that Sunday is particularly set aside for all of these things.

Family and friends

Sunday is a day for relationships with people, as well as with God.

Let me make quite clear what I do *not* mean by that. I read a letter in a magazine from a young married woman. She and her husband worked all week, then spent the weekend visiting their many friends and relations. Sometimes they would go together, sometimes there were so many people to cover that they had to split up. And they were in danger of splitting up permanently because they hardly ever saw each other, and certainly not alone.

There is a lot to be said for visiting friends or relations, and if that is what gives you the greatest pleasure, go ahead and do it. On the other hand, it can become a chore, and if you spread yourself too thinly it can get in the way of the most important relationships. Not all visits can be avoided, but most people will understand if you explain honestly that, for instance, you and your spouse are not getting any time together—or you and your parents, or you and your children, or whoever it is.

The length of time you spend with others is, of course, not the only consideration. I hesitate to use the phrase 'quality time' because it has been much abused over recent years. It's possible to make an excuse for not spending more time with someone, using the argument that you are still giving them 'quality time'. But quality really is more important than quantity. You can spend all day with a companion and virtually ignore each other or you can spend half an hour and really engage. Busy Sundays may not be the occasion for spending any length of time together but you can make the effort to bring in that quality. It does take an effort but, like worship—like the relationship with God, you get out what you put in. It may take a lot of persistence even to get through to some people, but those relationships can be the most rewarding in the end.

Then, do not be afraid to put your feet up and relax if you want to. We tend to be so full of the Protestant work ethic that we think we are sinning if we are not doing something, particularly something useful. Certainly, being lazy is no good thing, but most people today do not have time to be lazy. If we are not working, we feel we should be making constructive use of our leisure time. We end up trying to enjoy ourselves because we feel guilty if we do not. That is totally counter-productive.

I say again, relax. Sunday is the day off. If you do not want to do anything, don't. Of course, this entails a proviso that we should be careful not to leave all the work to someone else. On the other hand, if we have to be constantly busy we may well be making more work for them too.

A good rest can alleviate the desert feeling in three ways. Firstly, you may be feeling that way partly because you are over-tired and over-stressed. You need to get your energy back. It has been repeatedly shown that taking a planned rest after lunch, rather than just slogging on, makes workers much more productive. Let yourself recharge your batteries. It will do wonders for your mental as well as your physical well-being.

Secondly, many people rush round so fast that their imagination is drowned out by all the traffic noise. Very few people can live a totally prosaic existence and be happy. Daydreams can open up whole new worlds that we could never travel to in real life and perhaps would not want to. (Being James Bond in your imagination is much safer than being James Bond in real life, if such a thing were possible.) And it is a lot cheaper than having a holiday.

If we let our imagination drift, it may conjure up the answers to problems. How many times have you thought very hard about something and come up with nothing, only to have the answer pop into your brain when you are thinking about something else entirely? You may find solutions to problems you did not know you had.

Thirdly, the other thing that can easily get drowned out by too much activity is the voice of God. We know that God can speak to us any time and any place, whatever we are doing. But which is more likely: hearing a still, small voice when we are trying to keep everyone amused, or hearing a still, small voice when we are sitting in an arm-chair doing nothing in particular? I am not talking about sitting with bated breath waiting for a 'word', just keeping half an ear open in case there is a message for you. You never know; remember, Samuel was not expecting it either.

One last tip: fresh air and sleep are good for us. It might sound trite but they can make a huge difference to how you feel, clearing the head and making things look brighter. They may not solve anything but, let's face it, we can use all the help we can get. Sunday might be the best day to fit in that fresh air and sleep but every day would be better.

It is not easy to put the Sabbath back where it belongs. The world does not make it easy. It seems odd that we should have to work at having a day off, but that is the way it is. We need Sunday as an oasis even if we cannot yet get out of the desert. We need to recognize its holiness as a day set apart, but we need to also recognize that it is set apart for us. It is the chance to get our whole selves back in order. If we cannot achieve the kind of Sabbath that we need, we can at least take a few steps towards it. Once again, we have to be realistic, but God is waiting to back up any moves we make.

On Friday evenings Jews wish each other 'Sabbath peace' for next day. 'Sabbath peace' to you. *Shabbat shalom.*

CHAPTER 8

JETHRO'S ADVICE

Read Exodus 18:13–27 and Numbers 11:16–30.

OK, I'll confess. I am not the best person to be writing a chapter on leadership. Most of my leadership experience comes from being president of the college worship group two years running (no one else wanted the job), although, as I have already said, I am a lay preacher and have been a church steward.

So why am I including this chapter? Because I fear that those in leadership positions might be especially vulnerable to the exile experience. At the very least, they are as likely to get it as anyone else. If they do, it can affect a lot of other people; and if the leader knows this, it can leave them in a very isolated position, not daring to be themselves or help themselves in case they damage others' morale.

I am writing this with a view to church leaders, because I know more about that than leadership in other spheres. If you are a leader in some other situation, I hope you can find something to use here.

It is also true that leaders may be able to spot and help others going through the desert, although leaders who are still going through it may be blind to it in others or feel themselves unable to cope with someone else's problems.

God in all this

First of all, we need to remember that, as leaders, we are not actually in charge. God is. He gives us some responsibility but he also shoulders the burden alongside us. We may feel we are carrying other people but ultimately, God is carrying us.

Moses was a leader with the kind of authority that few of us can imagine. He was the direct channel between God and God's people. And he got worse flak than your average Prime Minister gets these days. Nothing happened without somebody complaining or someone else challenging his authority. Even his own family did it, despite the fact that Aaron and Miriam had both been given a measure of authority by God. If the Israelites had had walls, they would have been covered in graffiti: 'Moses go home'; 'Come back Pharaoh, all is forgiven'; 'What is this manna stuff, anyway?'

Even so, they expected Moses to do all the work. Not only did he speak to God for them—and that must have been a strain in itself, considering what they got up to—but he also had to act as judge and arbitrator for the whole community. We are not talking about a few dozen people here, we are talking of thousands; and if they were as quarrelsome among themselves as they were against God, then it must have been a never-ending task to sort them out.

There are actually two stories about how God solved the problem. The second involves direct divine intervention, the first some good old-fashioned common sense. Each of them raises some interesting points. We will look at Jethro—and common sense—first.

The father-in-law

Jethro is an interesting character. He is a priest of a foreign nation but the Bible speaks of him with no disapproval. Presumably the god of whom he was priest was Israel's God. He is a leader in his own right and he not only spots Moses' problem straight away, he comes up with a solution—the appointment of more judges—and gets it put into practice. He is a very useful person to have around.

What is Jethro's motive? He does not appear to be the domineering type. Perhaps he has had these kinds of problems himself and was either given the same advice or had to work it out. Almost certainly there is an element of compassion. He can see the mess his son-in-law has got himself into. He can guess what a miserable life his daughter and grandsons are going to have if the mess is not sorted out soon. So he sorts it out.

Advice can be a pain in the neck. It does not always matter whether the advice is right or wrong; the most important thing can be whether or not it is offered kindly and helpfully. Most people know that, though we all slip up occasionally. Unfortunately, there are people who never seem to realize that they are giving advice in an unhelpful way. Sometimes you wonder if they do it on purpose. It might be a leader's job to explain the problem to them tactfully. Or it might be the leader who is the culprit.

A group of young people had been taking services for some time when the clergyman responsible for them changed. The previous gentleman had offered occasional comments, pointed out suitable hymns and answered questions, but generally let the young people get on with it and learn their stuff. The new one told the group (by now very experienced) exactly what they should put in their services, including the sermons, with no expectation that they might have any ideas of their own, let alone anything worth hearing. Consequently, the group always listened to the first clergyman and not to the second, even when he might have had something useful to say.

Jethro, as father-in-law, is in a position of family seniority even if Moses is the leader of Israel. He does not appear to make much attempt to be tactful. So why does Moses accept what he says straight off? Is it simply that he knows Jethro is usually right? Has he been thinking along the same lines but needs confirmation from somebody else? We do not know, but the advice is given and taken with a good grace. Both sides need to respect the other person.

If we give advice, is it because we really want to help or because we think we know all about the subject? If we reject advice, is it because the advice is wrong or because we do not like being told what to do? The young people in the situation above ended up rejecting advice without listening to it, because they were fed up with the person giving it.

Jethro had a clear view of what was going on and concern for the person he was advising. Moses had the humility not to feel put out when advice was offered.

Humility

Here is a word we do not hear very often today, even in the church—humility. And when we do hear it, we tend to misunderstand it. Humility does not mean being too scared or too glum to speak up for yourself. It does not mean thinking that you have nothing worthwhile to contribute. It means having a proper view of your place in the universe. Compared to God we are dust, but God loves us and that makes us important. We are all equally important because God loves us all equally, with no exceptions.

False humility prevents a lot of good advice from being offered, which is even worse than advice being offered in the wrong way. If it is never heard, it cannot be acted upon. If it is put wrongly, it might cause initial irritation but the hearer can still act on it later.

By false humility, I do not mean hypocrisy. I mean the kind of humility that has us pushing ourselves down, down, down all the time—which is not at all what God wants. It can make us wilfully disregard our talents and achievements even when we know we have done something good. True humility, on the other hand, lets us hear the words for what they are, even if the other person delivers them badly. If Moses had thought that following Jethro's advice would damage his standing, he would have continued as he was behaving and probably burnt himself out, which was *not* what God wanted.

This relates to the exile experience in two ways. Directly, I wonder how many people in the wilderness are suffering from some kind of burn-out that might have been prevented if they had listened—or if someone else had spoken up with what common sense, or God, had told them. Indirectly, how many people are suffering because false humility tells them they are of no value?

So, how do you give advice and how do you take it? From whom do you take it? The leader's attitude can set the tone for the whole group.

Certain people may be noted for giving wise advice or being expert on a particular subject. These people usually get a hearing. But life in general, and God in particular, show that the most surprising people may have a contribution to make. Look at all the people God chose for special tasks. Several of them replied, 'Who, me?' (Moses) and many more had people saying, 'Who, him?' (Jesus included). And some probably said, 'Who, her?' every time God's choice was a woman (for example, Deborah, the only female Judge, Judges 4—5).

Some people get ignored in life, either through prejudice or because they are backward in putting themselves forward, and it is part of a leader's job to spot these people and bring them out. If this can be done, it is good for the individual concerned and it is good for the whole congregation. Everyone is a valuable resource. If some people are being blocked from coming forward, not only is that a waste, it may also send them into their own exile experience if they are not in one already. The church should be particularly open and welcoming—but we all know it does not always work that way.

The content of the message

Let us turn to the content of Jethro's message: 'delegate'.

A great many people these days are overworked, and this applies to leaders as much as to anyone else—leaders in certain circles, at any rate: in the Church, in voluntary organizations, and so on. There are quite a number of reasons for this but one significant reason is that some people find it hard to delegate. Not everyone does—we all know people who are more than happy to let others do the job—but some people, like Moses, find it very hard.

For a start, there may simply not be anyone to whom they can delegate. The harvest is great but the workers are few (Matthew

9:37). If this is the case, there is little you can do except to get rid of any inessential chores.

Sometimes, though, the workers appear few because people have been overlooked. Some people are not obvious; some are downright invisible. Yet many people have skills or talents that they would be happy to donate, given the right encouragement. Such people need reassurance that they can do the job, that their contribution will be valued and that they will not be given a hard time if they later have to give up or want to move on to something else. Sadly, the Church, like other organizations, does not always provide this kind of positive environment; and leaders, clergy and lay, are sometimes (often?) responsible. Then again, if the leaders are not getting this kind of encouragement themselves, it is hard for them to provide it to others. It takes a great deal of grace.

There are a number of other reasons for not delegating. One very 'British' one is that we do not like to ask. We do not want to bother people. It is true that on occasions it is easier to do something ourselves than to try and find someone else to do it. On other occasions the problem is simply reticence.

Some people do not delegate because they do not feel they should, because they feel they are letting people down if they do not do at least twice their official job description. If you can cope with that, fair enough. There is no shortage of work to be done. But you do not have to do it all yourself. If you are suffering by it, or are being prevented from doing something more important, you need to offload. Some church denominations, like some secular organizations, have always been better at sharing out the jobs. On the other hand, many people still consider that there are certain jobs that the clergy should do, or that are the responsibility of particular office holders, despite the increase in administration in the church and the general fall in the number of clergy.

Frankly, it is not our expectations or other people's that matter. It is God's. The most important question is always what God wants from us in a given situation. And the answer to that question is not going to be that we run ourselves into the ground. What good does that do anyone? The more tired we are, the less productive we are. So again, step back. See what really needs doing. Get help. Even Jesus did not do all the work himself. He had twelve disciples, and even sent out 72 to preach on one occasion (Luke 10:1).

Then there are people who, consciously or subconsciously, like to think they are indispensable. Nothing will get done if they are not around—at least, not if they have anything to do with it.

This is pride, though it can be quite unconscious. It can also stop other people from showing their gifts. I heard a story about an organist who refused to let anyone else touch the church organ. *He* was the organist, nobody else. He was quite outraged when he was asked to teach one of the children in the congregation. What kind of impact did that have on that child—both musically and spiritually—not to mention her parents, other members of the congregation and of course the man's own soul? Indeed, most churches I know are desperately short of organists. The impact of this man's pride—conscious or unconscious—may have spread further than he ever knew.

God and the unexpected

There is a similar story to the one about Jethro a little later on in the Bible (Numbers 11:16–30). Moses is fed up, so God gets him to bring the elders to meet him and he confers on them some of the gift he has given to Moses. They start to prophesy. I bet that was a shock for everyone, themselves included. Then things get even weirder when two of the elders who had not gone with the others start prophesying inside the camp. Nobody knows what to do. Joshua asks Moses if he should shut them up. Moses has the wisdom not to be jealous, to know that this is God's doing—never mind that no one expected it.

It is not so much that the two men in question were a surprising choice to receive this gift. After all, they were already elders. What caused the trouble was that the situation was outside the norm. If God gave someone a special blessing, he did it up a mountain or at the Tent of the Meeting. He did not do it in the middle of the camp, in the middle of everyday life. Only this time, of course, he did.

We get used to certain structures. They may not be the old way of doing things, they might be reforms we have brought in ourselves. They may very well be what God wants—most of the time. But human beings are only flexible up to a point, unlike God. He knows this. He works with it, but sometimes he wants us to go outside the established structures, just once or for a total change. Sometimes, perhaps, he even asks for a change so that we will not get stuck in a rut.

It can be hard to let go of the way we have done things since we were children. It can be even harder to let go of the changes we have brought in, that we have carefully nurtured. Yet we do need to do that sometimes. We need to fix our priorities by focusing on God.

Personal spirituality

Another question: how many Christian leaders do not spend enough time with God? Time is at a premium. There is a great deal to do. Prayer time and worship tend to get squeezed unless a determined effort is made. Of course, many people make that effort but others do not, although it is vital. Perhaps you know the anonymous poem that starts:

> *I got up early one morning and rushed right into the day;*
> *I had so much to accomplish that I didn't have time to pray.*

It is a little well-worn but it does make a good point. We know that whether we pray or not will make no difference to the blessings that God offers us. But it *will* make a difference to how open we are to receive them. It will make a difference to whether we are calm or flustered. It will make a difference to whether we know what God wants for the day.

And do not forget: Jesus often went away by himself to pray. I would guess that that is what he was doing for those forty days in the wilderness (Mark 1:12–13). Certainly we know that on other occasions he spent the day or night in prayer (Luke 6:12). I am all in favour of getting a good night's sleep, as I said earlier, but spending longer times alone with God can be a good idea. Certainly many people find it useful. This is where conventional 'wilderness spirituality' can be of importance, spending time on your own to be with God, perhaps on an organized retreat.

As for worship, preachers or worship leaders face a particular problem. While the rest of the congregation is (you hope) getting the benefit of all your hard work, you are too busy planning your next move to approach God at all.

I find this when I am preaching and it used to worry me. Now I concentrate on three simple coping strategies. When leading the prayers, my main concern is to say the right words for the congregation. However, between times I can make a series of short, silent 'Help!' prayers to cover each phase of the service.

Secondly, I concentrate my own worship in the hymns. It is very tempting to spend most of the hymns getting ready for what comes next. However, these days I will myself to relax and let go, to really worship God in those few minutes. I find it can be very refreshing and fulfilling. Sometimes I even pick the hymns more for my benefit than the congregation's, though I never choose anything that I feel would be detrimental to their worship! The refreshment I get from this does more for the quality of the service than would be achieved by having my papers in order a few seconds earlier.

Thirdly, what do you do immediately after the service? There is a great temptation to dash to the back of the church in order to shake hands with the departing congregation. Indeed, some of them flee like frightened rabbits and it takes a considerable turn of speed to get to the door before them.

Most people consider it part of the preacher's job to speak to people as they leave but I am not sure that some people want to be spoken to. If they do, can they not wait two minutes for you?

What I do at the end of the service is to sit down and have a moment's quiet prayer, generally along the lines of: 'Thank you that's over. I hope that was what you wanted.' And this is when I most often feel the blessing and renewal of energy that I need at that moment. It does not take long. If I miss a few people going out, that is unfortunate, but I think I communicate better with those who remain if I have prayed. I know I feel better myself.

Doubt

There may, however, be a more fundamental problem for preachers or other leaders—doubt. It can be a particular problem for those who have to stand up and proclaim what they hope to be God's word. You can chair a meeting on a human level without too much of a problem. In fact, apart from the prayers at the beginning and end, there is little difference between a Christian meeting and any other sort. Preaching and leading worship, on the other hand, are supposed to be inspired by God—even if most of the job is the hard slog of getting the words and hymn numbers together.

As leaders, we may find ourselves facing two main kinds of doubt —doubt in God and doubt in ourselves.

Nerves are natural when we have so great a responsibility. Apparently my grandfather, a preacher of many years' standing, could never eat his tea before an evening service. Are we up to the task? Not on our own, no.

Remember what God said to the apostle Paul: 'My strength is made perfect in weakness' (2 Corinthians 12:9). If I was Paul I would be tempted to reply, 'Thanks a lot, I'd rather be strong', but in actual fact our weakness lets us off the hook. We can never be strong enough to deal with everything we meet in life. We do not have to be. We do what we can and God will do the rest. This applies to our own lives and whatever responsibility we have for the lives of others. So relax a little. Pray about it. Do what you can but do not take the world on your shoulders. That is not your job. (Try listening to the Beatles' song 'Hey, Jude' occasionally!)

Remember, God appreciates our best efforts even if no one else does. And his is the only opinion that matters.

Then there is doubt in God. You find lots of people in the Bible who doubt themselves—Moses, Gideon, the psalmist and many of the prophets—but it is rather hard for people to doubt God. At least, it is hard to doubt the existence of God. But plenty of people have doubts about what he is doing or whether he is any use. Look at the Israelites: they are brought out of Egypt with miracles and five minutes later they do not believe that God can supply them with water (Exodus 15:22–25). They carry on like that throughout their Old Testament history, constantly turning to other gods.

But it is not just the masses, or those who actively do evil, who doubt God. (Curiously, the great villain Ahab never expresses any doubt about God's existence.) Many of the Bible's most famous names do too: Elijah when he is chased out after the riot on Mount Carmel; Jeremiah, frequently (Jeremiah 12:1–4); even Moses. How often does Moses ask God to kill him because the whole thing has just degenerated into a mess? For instance, in Numbers 11:10–15, just before the second reading at the head of this chapter, he says, 'If this is how you are going to treat me, put me to death right now—if I have found favour in your eyes—and do not let me face my own ruin.'

Doubting God and doubting his existence are not so far apart in practice. Indeed, the second can be easier to deal with than the first. If there is no God, that explains a lot. If there is a God, it leaves us with a lot of questions—questions that need honest answers.

I can only offer a few practical suggestions, not deep theology—though deep theology might be a good start. I know some people think that reading theology tends to undermine faith but this is a very unfair generalization. It depends what you read and how you read it. Just because something is modern, radical or complex, it is not more likely to be true than something simple or traditional—and vice versa. We need to judge what we read on the evidence it presents, whether it is internally consistent and whether it accords with other things we hold to be reliable.

It is important to have an informed faith, particularly for preachers. We may not pass on everything we have learned, as a sermon does not lend itself to complex exposition except under certain circumstances, but preaching should be like the proverbial iceberg or like a good novel. If an author has thought their book through properly, it will be set in a much broader world than ever makes it on to the page. They will know what their main characters like to eat and how they behave if they go shopping, what life was like when they grew up. None of this may ever reach the reader but it informs everything that the characters do and say and gives them depth. Just so with a preacher and their sermon.

Yet younger preachers in particular can be afraid of learning too much in case it damages what they already believe. I have seen some young people go through painful times as they cope with new information that causes them to question some things they held as absolute. It happened to me when I was taking A-level RE and in hindsight I am glad it did. In the end it strengthened my faith, though I also learnt that faith is a work in progress, that you have to live with doubts.

Modern faith does co-exist with doubt for many, if not most, people. I suspect that it has always been that way. Look at some of the psalms that express both great faith and great doubt. But this is difficult for preachers if they want to speak honestly. It is necessary to get things clear in your head. What do you believe? What can you say without compromising your integrity?

Some people might feel that they have to keep saying the same things they have always said, even when they no longer believe them. I do not think that this is good for either preacher or congregation. Congregations can be as good at reading the preacher as they are the text, and may well pick up on any dishonesty. Is that good for their faith? This struggle with faith may put you in the desert—it may be happening *because* you are in the desert—and others may be edged towards that desert if they do not think they can find honesty in the Church.

It is better to concentrate on what you do believe, even if that is not much. Say what you can honestly say and leave out the rest. If it feels right, share your doubts with the congregation. They may identify with the doubts and you can work through them together. You may be addressing a great need that they have, or they may have the answers that you are looking for. (Why not? Why should preachers not learn from congregations?) Even if neither of these is the case, the congregation may well be more sympathetic than you expect. Besides anything else, people appreciate being treated as adults. In time, you may come back to beliefs you formerly held or find yourself with new ones that are stronger. The congregation may support you in this time and then you can really get down to preaching, to supporting them.

If you do not feel that you can go on as a leader, then do not force yourself and make the situation worse. It is best to admit the problem before any real damage is done to yourself or your congregation. It is also better to think of taking time off rather than giving up completely but this may not be possible. It is a big step, but if you honestly feel it is the right one, take it. God may have other things for you to do or, at the least, it may preserve your spiritual health. If you are not sure, do not be afraid to talk the issues through with someone. That someone may or may not be another preacher. The most important thing is that they are someone with whom you feel comfortable. But in the long run, the decision is between you and God, so do not let yourself be pushed in any way that you do not want to go. People have to respect your point of view if it is sincerely held.

Whether you decide to take time off or not, I say again, go back to basics. Go back to what you know you believe, however small or simple, then build from the ground up. A minimal but honest faith is better than all the pretence you can muster about what you think you ought to believe. It will not fool God.

If in the end you find you do not believe in God, even that must be admitted. It is a better starting point for faith and for life than any amount of pretended belief. However, if you did not believe in him at all, I doubt you would be reading this book.

People need people

Family can make all the difference to your life—and theirs—but can become sadly neglected in favour of 'God's work'.

Let's get this perfectly straight: family relationships are important to God. He created them. Genesis starts with a couple who soon develop into a family, however wrong their relationships might go. God frequently works through families—Abraham comes complete with wife, nephew and eventually sons. At least in theory, the Israelites were a family. It is no accident that Jesus is described as God's Son. We—and the Israelites—are frequently described as God's children. For all the verses saying that you should put God before family, there are a dozen telling you to look after that family. Paul says that anyone who cannot take care of their natural family is not fit to look after the family of the Church (see 1 Timothy 3—although first-century concepts of the family are rather different from ours). Yet Christian workers do sometimes neglect their families. I know of a family where the parents had effectively abandoned their children to go off and do missionary work overseas. Two of the children ran wild and one was totally unable to cope with normal social interaction. It did the children no good, it did the reputation of the Church no good and you have to wonder if the missionary work did anyone any good under such circumstances.

That is an extreme example but how many families get squeezed under the pressure of work? Clergy spouses and clergy children in particular have outside expectations put on them because of the family they belong to. They need more help, not less.

Mostly the problem is pressure of time. There is so much to be done, and if the work is God's work… Well, is it always? If someone is getting hurt because of this work, we are left with a very big question mark. God always comes first, but what does it do for God's reputation if those we love most are getting hurt because of what we regard as his will?

In the end, the solutions are the same as for many of the problems I have discussed in previous chapters: prioritize, ask for help, and pray. Indeed, improving relations with your family may be the solution to other problems. For example, while some young people might want to run as far away as possible if they have a clergy parent, others would feel extremely flattered if that parent entrusted them with an important job in the church.

Finally, remember that we are not really the leaders. Like the elders with Moses, we actually follow. We follow God. That is a great responsibility in some ways but in others it takes a weight off our shoulders. We do not have to take responsibility for everything. Do not ever feel guilty if you feel lost in the desert. Offer that to God and perhaps he will make you a true leader, one who leads others out of the wilderness.

CHAPTER 9

MANNA

Read Exodus 16.

The Israelites really were an ungrateful lot. When they looked back at their life in Egypt, did they thank God for rescuing them from slavery? *No.* It was all 'You should have left us there. We had pots of food. Literally. Meat, veg, anything we wanted. Now what are we going to eat?'

Moses rolled his eyes to heaven and God said: 'I'll give them bread. I'll give them plenty. I'll make it rain bread.'

And he did. Every morning when they got up, the ground was covered in bread. They just had to go and pick it up. In fact, they not only got quantity but quality. As my sister has pointed out, manna was not bread, it was Frosties—delicate, crispy wafers that did look like frost on the ground. In effect, God said 'Let them eat cake' and provided the cake. It was far better than anything that they would have had in Egypt, where people lived on bread and beer. And the Israelites were still not happy.

Wanting it all

We are told we live in an aspirational society. What that really means is that people want things, and on those terms every society in history has been aspirational. These days, there are more things around us to want, but whether that makes the problem any worse I do not know.

It is not entirely true to say that things cannot make us happy. If I just look around my desk I can see various things that have made me happy or still do—an Indian brass vase that was a present from some visitors; a bellumnite fossil I found on Skegness beach; a little plastic Snoopy dressed as a pirate, which reminds me of a novel I started and have not yet had time to finish. And it is not just cheap things. The house, the car and even the video recorder (none of them actually mine) all contribute substantially to my happiness. A surprise gift, a bargain or something useful—they all brighten up our day. Things in themselves are not bad. Things can be a gift from God as much as less material blessings.

So while the enjoyment of what we have will never get us out of the wilderness, it can give us a boost along the way. Play with your new toy!

The problem is that we are never satisfied. We get one thing and we want another. We see an advert and we are seduced. Even worse, we see what someone else has and we get jealous. We are made to think that we are not normal if we behave any other way. We are only of value if we have valuable things.

And we know that is a load of rubbish. Very few people on this planet really believe that possessions are what make somebody important. We have a higher sense of values inside us. It is part of the image of God in us that we all share, Christian or not. We know that people are more important than things. Most civilizations punish crimes against people more harshly than crimes against property, which gives a good indication of a society's values. We know that what we do, what we are, is more important than what we own. We even know—if we push ourselves—that we can be happy without much in the way of material possessions. We may have seen people do it; we may have given things up ourselves.

But the world keeps telling us otherwise and it makes us discontented. This concentration on the material pushes us towards an inner emptiness and that wilderness feeling.

It's time to get a sense of proportion. The Israelites kept looking back to what they had seen in Egypt. Whether or not they actually had access to all the foods they describe is a moot point. They knew those foods were there, anyway. Perhaps they were also looking forward to the Promised Land of milk and honey. Things that we might get one day are much more tempting than things that we have no hope of getting our hands on. We might never get that Ferrari, but the next model of car up from the one we own, that is another story...

But the fact is, the Israelites were doing very well for themselves. (Or rather, God was doing very well for them.) Most people at that time would have had an exceptionally boring diet. They would eat the same thing, day in, day out, just like the Israelites. However, they would not have the delicate, tasty manna. They would be eating un-leavened bread or some kind of porridge—flat and unappetizing. Many people in the world today live on a similar sort of diet. But the Israelites got bored with what they had.

How many times do you look at a perfectly good meal and wish you had something else?

We do. We get bored in spite of all the choice around us. Maybe it is *because* of all the choice around us. I am told that if you bring up a cat to eat only one type of food, they will not touch anything else that is put before them. If, on the other hand, you bring them up on a wide variety of foods and then start feeding them the same thing every day, they will go on hunger strike. Cats are a lot like people.

Once again, I am not trying to make anyone feel guilty. That will not help. There is a certain amount of sinfulness in always wanting something else but there is also a good deal of curiosity involved. Curiosity is normal and natural. Indeed, it is a good thing. It is a God-given trait to help us get on in the world and to make our lives richer. The human race would hardly have achieved anything without it.

Me, I'm curious. I am the sort of person who always orders the one thing on the menu that they do not know. Half the time I end up hating what arrives but the other fifty per cent makes up for it. Whatever curiosity is, it is not a problem. The problem is when we let it run out of control or, more to the point, when we let our desire to see what is round the next corner stop us from enjoying what is here.

A balancing act

First we have to make proper comparisons. We may not have as much as some people we know, but by world standards anyone reading this book is probably rich. Few in this country need worry where their next meal is coming from or how to keep a roof over their heads. Most have enough to enjoy and indulge themselves a little.

You can take three attitudes to that. You can say, 'Yes but I'm not as rich as so-and-so and I won't be happy until I am.' Or you can say, 'That's awful. I feel so guilty', and sit around feeling bad about it. Or you can enjoy what you have but be prepared to share when the need arises—as it constantly does.

Which of those is the most healthy? Which is going to make you happiest?

I think of John Paul Getty Junior, whose family's wealth appears to have caused them nothing but unhappiness. He seems to have reversed that trend by giving away to galleries, museums and other good causes. Most of us could never dream of being that rich but little gestures make us feel better as well as benefiting the people we are helping. You see the smile on someone's face and you know that it was worth the cost, or you give away something precious to you and know you will no longer have to worry about it because you have done the right thing. Let's face it, possessions are a worry. What if I drop the vase? What if I spill coffee on the keyboard? What if I get burgled? Jesus told us to build up treasure in heaven rather than on earth (Matthew 6:19–21). It is safe there; nothing can damage it and we can enjoy it here and now or in the future.

What is treasure in heaven? It's the happiness we give to others; good deeds done in secret; the love that grows in our hearts. No one can steal or damage those.

Second, we have to remember that enjoying the world and owning it are not the same thing. It is good to explore the world. The things that God made are good. The things that people have made are, by and large, good. But that does not mean we have to acquire them. We can get into the frame of mind that acquisition is all that matters. In truth, the important thing is the good that that item can do for you. We can go racing after the next new object of desire, but it is more fun to enjoy what we already have.

I have possessions put away in cupboards because they are too good to put out. Then I am afraid to take them out and look at them just in case they have somehow been damaged. And I go on acquiring other possessions and putting them away, until the cupboards are over-flowing with junk. Is that sensible? No, it is not.

Third, we should remember that a good way to enjoy our possessions is to share them. Having a party is much more fun than eating alone. There are several reasons why sharing is fun. We can make people happy or help those who need help. But it is also a good way of building friendship and fellowship. I am not talking about buying friends. Everyone knows that that does not work. On the other hand, everyone is attracted to those of a generous nature. People who share what they have usually share themselves, and sharing is often part of doing things together, an important element to friendship. God may well have blessed us with a lot, but if he did, it is so that we can bless others *and* bless ourselves.

Fourth, in the long run we need to know that material things are not important. We probably do know that in our heads, just as the Israelites probably knew that it did not matter what they ate, as long as they did eat.

Could we give up everything we own if we had good enough reason? We admire people who do, but could we? Or are we like all those ancient civilizations who did not just want wealth in their lifetimes, they wanted to take it with them—so people were buried surrounded by possessions. (Of course, they are a boon to archaeologists!)

Daniel

Could we refuse the riches of this world if they were handed to us on a plate? That is effectively what happens to Daniel and his friends at the beginning of the book that bears his name (Daniel 1). They were literally exiles, kidnapped from their homes. Then they were offered a very good deal. Serve the king and they could live in the lap of luxury. Daniel and his friends had been the élite: they were used to luxury. Life was merely returning to what was more like normality. And they had no problem serving the king. If they were running the Babylonian empire, they could do a good job of it. They could do it God's way.

However, they did have one very specific problem. The meat they were given to eat had almost certainly been sacrificed to idols. To eat it would be unfaithful to God. So they decided to go vegetarian.

That was a very unusual choice to make in those days. The diet of the rich was almost entirely meat-based. The main reason for not eating meat would be that you did not have any. To eat only vegetables would be a loss of status as well as diet. It was a real sacrifice, if you will excuse the pun.

There are several things to note in passing. For one thing, Daniel and his friends did not go over the top. They did not decide that all the gifts that they were being offered were evil. They only turned down the one that threatened to compromise them and get in the way of their relationship with God.

Also, they were careful that no one was hurt by their actions. They asked their overseer for a trial run and were prepared to give up if there was a chance that he would get into trouble because of them. Religious principles are fine but God is more interested in people. You hear stories about people who apparently make great sacrifices but the real costs are paid by others. In real life, matters are often not clear-cut. It can be difficult to decide what will be for someone's long-term good and genuine mistakes are made. The principle, however, remains the same: if you are making sacrifices, it should really be you who makes them. That is the way Jesus did it.

Lastly, the friends were more than rewarded for what they did. They became the healthiest, best-looking men in the group (Daniel 1:15).

Life in this day and age is not usually that simple. Sometimes a good action does automatically bring benefits, expected or unexpected. Sometimes quite the opposite happens and doing what is right only brings trouble. Most often, the result lies somewhere in the middle: what we do is largely ignored.

But God does not forget our good actions.

It is very true that we cannot buy our way into heaven, like the woman in the song 'Stairway to Heaven', but it does please God when we act as people who really are made in his image. There's treasure in heaven again.

Any one of the young men in Babylon could have done the same as Daniel's group. Maybe some of them thought about it. Only four did it. Only four are remembered.

What would we do under those circumstances? Take the easy way or stand out from the crowd?

For best results follow maker's instructions

Let's go back to the question of manna and the other problem the Israelites had with it—obeying the Maker's instructions.

God was pretty specific in his instructions (Exodus 16:4–5, 15–20, 23–27): 'Six days a week you gather it. You do not keep any overnight except on the sixth day because there will not be any on the seventh.' Just two things to remember, and some people still managed to get them wrong.

Relying on God can be difficult. Relying on God for material provision seems to be beyond most people. Jesus told us not to worry about food and clothes and the like, but to worry about the Kingdom of God (Luke 12:22–31). The truth is, we might worry about the Kingdom of God some of the time but we worry much more about our bodily needs.

This is not entirely surprising. We do not want to go bust, nor is it part of God's plan for us to be reckless with money—but to trust God to provide when circumstances suggest that there is a problem takes an awful lot of faith.

You do hear stories about people who run missions and orphanages and who always have a donation coming in right at the last moment, for exactly the right amount. Half of us thinks 'How wonderful' but we can sometimes have a sneaking suspicion that their financial planning was at fault.

There is nothing wrong with being sensible. Good financial management is a virtue, whether with your own money or an institution's. Far more churches rely on capable property stewards than on miracles. Do not worry.

Worry and sense

'Do not worry' is easier said than done. I have already said that I am a worrier. I have lain awake at night wondering if my grant would stretch to the end of term (when there were still such things as grants) or whether I would have enough left from my giro cheque to get into town and sign on again. I still have similar worries. They contribute to the wilderness. What do I do about them?

I usually start by telling myself not to be so stupid. That rarely works. I might try distracting myself, with a daydream or something else. That sometimes works. The best thing is to ask myself two questions: 'How likely is it?' and 'What will the consequences be?'

If you add up all the relevant factors, it usually comes out that complete financial ruin is rather unlikely. This is especially true if you have managed to avoid it in the past. Think of all the pluses instead of all the minuses.

Then think what the consequences would actually be: complete ruin or a spot of belt-tightening? What can we do without? Might it do us good to go without a few things?

Each different set of circumstances produces a different set of calculations. However, most of them will result in something we can actually live with. We might need to shift our expectations but we are unlikely to starve.

When we are thinking straight, then we make an effort of will to trust God. Trust is always a matter of will, though our past history can be a help. We may already have evidence that we can trust God to look after us—different evidence for each person.

We sometimes think that worrying is being realistic. In fact it is more like focusing on the negative and ignoring the positive. It wastes energy, like trying to gather manna on the Sabbath. It distracts us from doing something better. So stamp on or reason away worries as soon as they come up. Be prepared for the best as well as the worst.

And once again, pray. Pray for the right outcome. Pray to trust God. Pray to relax.

Manna is great. Plenty in our lives is great. This is a good world and we are generally doing very well in it, even if our neighbours are doing better. But this world is not the be-all and end-all. We are intended for something better. So we have to sit lightly to the material world, enjoy it but not become obsessed with it, or the good might get in the way of the best and trap us in the desert.

CHAPTER 10

WATER

Read Exodus 15:22–27, Exodus 7:1–7 and Numbers 20:1–13.

Water is a very powerful image in the Bible. That's hardly surprising, as water is still a very powerful subject in the Middle East. Everyone needs water to live and it often seems that there is not enough to go round. Some well-informed people think that the next Middle Eastern war will be fought over water rather than oil.

Either way, it is water that causes the most problems for the Israelites. Their first complaints, within three days of crossing the Red Sea, are about the bitter water at Marah. They do not have much faith that God will provide, in spite of experience.

We have covered the Israelites' complaints fairly thoroughly. This chapter takes a slightly different, more metaphorical tack. Let us look at the theme of water and dryness.

Water has always been equated directly with life. We would die much more quickly without air than water but the process of breathing was not really understood until a few centuries ago. Water can be seen and felt. It is regarded as vital throughout every culture. Abundance of water means abundance of life. Drought or desert means restriction of life and the threat of death.

We have already established that we are in the desert rather than the land of milk and honey. We are feeling that our lives are restricted.

We are not getting as much out as we should. Maybe we even feel we are dying or dead inside. Where do we go for water?

If you are a Christian, you ought to be able to guess the answer—to the Living Water. To Christ.

Living Water

Jesus describes himself as the Living Water to a woman making the long, regular walk from her village to the local well (John 4). She jumps at the chance to have such water 'on tap'. Wouldn't you? No more heavy jars to carry two or three times a day. Much more energy. Much more time. Maybe she could help her neighbours out. Water on tap, with no need ever to be thirsty again, would be a Godsend—literally. She really wants this.

With two thousand years of hindsight, we know that she mis-understood. But if anyone thinks she is being shallow, try her life. Try living without tap water, flush toilets, washing machines and so on. Think of the inconvenience, the extra work and the health hazards. Our water has been cut off a great many times in the last year because the water company are re-laying the pipes. On and off, on and off, it has been a real nuisance—but we always knew that it would come back in a few hours or so. It is a luxury the woman at the well would barely have been able to imagine.

With hindsight, we know that Jesus was not talking about H_2O. He said on another occasion that he came so that we might have life in abundance. That is what the Living Water provides, just as ordin-ary water does in a more limited way. Jesus offers God within ourself, the power of the universe on tap, just as water causes grass to spring up from the earth.

'Life in abundance.' I suppose that could sound like a threat if your life is lousy: lousiness going on for ever and ever and ever, amen. What a horrible thought. But Jesus was speaking qualitatively rather than quantitatively. You get up in the morning to bright sunshine, knowing that you can spend the whole day with the one you love at your favourite place on earth. He means that kind of life, in feeling if not in any literal sense.

Another picture might be like this. My mother has been to Israel on at least five occasions but with a gap of around twenty years between the second and third trips. What really struck her when she went back was how green everything had become. There were flowers and crops everywhere. Even around the Dead Sea the salt was being flushed from the soil and palms were being planted. She was seeing life out of dead ground, brought about by water—and a lot of hard work.

Of course, in the material world, there are political and ecological comebacks. In the material world, there is only so much water to go round. If it is in one place, it is not in another. If it is benefiting one person, it is not available for another. Just so, not all decisions turn out to be right, even if taken with the best of intentions. But if we appropriate the Living Water to ourselves, that will not cause an ecological crisis for someone else. There is more than enough to go round. There is an inexhaustible supply.

'Life in abundance.' The 'quality of life' is a phrase we hear a lot these days. Most of us know quality when we see it and we would rather buy quality than tat. It is more luxurious. It lasts longer. Yet while we might have surrounded ourselves with quality in material possessions, we may feel our lives to be of poor quality, pulling apart at the seams. They are dry and unappetizing. Maybe we feel that we are dried up. We need to come alive, like Japanese paper flowers that start as rolled-up pellets but expand in water to show their true beauty.

Jesus describes himself as having the Living Water (John 4:10). Later (John 7:38), he describes the Holy Sprit as Living Water. He is talking about direct access to God, God within us. This is not some kind of New Age concept of God being part of us. That leaves us on our own to sort out our problems, a lonely and depressing prospect. Living Water means quite the opposite. It is the power and love of God being there for us, where we need it, whenever we need it, right here, right now—not because we deserve it but because we need it, because without it we can be nowhere other than in the desert.

I shall say more about the presence of God in the next chapter, but what about abundant, fertile life?

An analogy

I'm a writer. You may have guessed that by the fact that you are reading my book. I can say that to people now, because I am actually writing words that get into print. But actually I have always been a writer. I have written odds and ends ever since I learnt how to write. I have started seven novels so far. Some of those were abandoned; some need to be restarted. Some I am theoretically still writing but have had to put them on hold until this book is finished. All were started in a great burst of enthusiasm that usually lasts for about three or four chapters. Then the problems set in.

It is not that I do not know where I am going with my novels. I usually have a fair idea of where I want the plot to end up. The problem is in deciding how to get there. I probably know two or three things I want to work into the story, but what exactly is going to happen *next*? And I have ideas for other stories that I want to get down on paper in case I lose them. Some days I look at my piece of paper, or my computer screen, and I just do not want to have anything to do with it. I do not feel like a writer. I do not feel creative. I just want to go and watch the television—only there's nothing worth watching.

'Life,' as Marvin the Paranoid Android used to say. 'Don't talk to me about life.'

It is odd that some of these problems seem to be caused by an over-abundance of good things. There are too many stories I could write, too many directions to take each story. There are difficulties— tiredness and lack of time being the main ones—but there is so much that is good, and I get too bogged down to see it. I get lost in the details instead of taking a step back. Maybe that is a time when I *should* go and watch television, if only so that I can tell myself that I can do better.

And the same goes for my life. Many people have a much worse life than I do. I am fully aware of that. It is not so much my circumstances that feel dead and dry. It is me.

Taking a drink

I guess this is going back to the beginning again (or rather, to Chapter Two). One person can cope with a set of circumstances that would throw someone else, then be floored by something that the other person would not find at all difficult. Different types of people, different problems. One God.

It strikes me that people only tend to go to God with certain types of problems. You have a spiritual problem, you pray about it. You have an illness, you pray about it. You have writer's block or stress or a vague sense of unease… Well, what do you do? Ask God, or let it ride? (I remember hearing one woman say we were prepared to pray about a cold but not about cancer. I rather think she got that the wrong way round. Would we bother God about a sore throat and a runny nose?)

Life with God is emphatically not 'pie in the sky when we die'. Eternal life is not about going on and on for ever, sitting on a cloud, playing that harp. It is about really living, before or after death. In a way, people like the ancient Egyptians were right to think that there is not such a great distinction between the two. They are simply two sides of the same door. Eternal life is about living to the full, being creative, sharing God's good gifts, whether we are writing a philosophical treatise, cooking lunch or painting the children's faces for a party—or, beyond death, praising God with all the company of heaven. It is not just about doing those things eternally but feeling the life of them internally, not just doing things but being truly alive. It means liberation to be ourselves, children of God.

The solutions to this dry, empty, desert experience are not simple, because it is so much a part of the human condition. First, we need to recognize that this feeling is a problem, not an inevitable consequence of being alive. Second, if we can, we should step back for a moment to look at the bigger picture. Third, we should pray. I keep saying it and I will keep on saying it—talk to God about your problem. Nothing is too big or too small, too diffuse or too specific for him. If it concerns us, it concerns him. Parents are like that—even human ones, mostly.

And we do have to *ask* for the Living Water. It is freely available, but it does not come out of the ground like a burst water-main. We have to ask Jesus for it, partly because we need to acknowledge that it is from him (John 4:10). We need to acknowledge him. He gives the gift, yet he also *is* the gift—one of those paradoxes of Christianity.

Then we can start to get everything else sorted out—all the things I have already discussed. We can take control of our thinking and stamp out or investigate negative thoughts. If such thoughts have any foundation, we should do something about them. That is something else that God can help us with. Align with God and you can make yourself think positive thoughts—not silly positive, but realistic positive; not pretending everything is right with the world, but taking a firm grasp on what is right. It will not make the bad feelings go away, but it will stop you making things worse for yourself (and everyone else). The good is just as real as the bad, even if we tend to forget that.

Do what you can—and do what you want to. Sometimes there is something we really need to do for our own sake or another's. Sometimes it is better for those around us if we do what we need to, rather than what we think we ought to do. Making the best use of our talents is good for us and for others. It is what God intends. It is also very often the most enjoyable thing (as God's intentions usually are). We need to have fun sometimes. All work and no play makes Jack rather less than human.

Rest. Get more sleep if you need it. Take a break and look at what you are doing. Take time off from it. Even abandon it if you have to. Perseverance is good but sometimes it just means throwing away effort when that could be spent more profitably elsewhere. Do things for other people but do things that will benefit you as well. God loves you just as much as anyone else.

Go and look for Jesus at the well. And read the next chapter.

CHAPTER 11

THE PILLAR

Read Exodus 13:20–22.

Except during the life of Jesus, it is rare for God to be visibly present. God is the unseen God, usually. Sometimes he 'dresses' as a human in order to visit people like Abraham (Genesis 18). There are other occasions where he appears as the *Shekinah*, the glowing cloud sometimes known as the 'glory of the Lord'. That was how he was seen at the dedication of Solomon's temple, so powerful a presence that the priests had to retreat (1 Kings 8:10–11). And then there is the fiery, cloudy pillar that led the Israelites around the desert for forty years.

In many ways, this fiery pillar is like the *Shekinah*. It is described in the same terms but it does not have the same impact on the Israelites. It is more of a symbol than an actual, concrete manifestation of God into the world of his creation. It indicates God's presence but it is not, in itself, God's presence. The Israelites did meet God face to face—or rather, they had the chance to—when he gave them the Law (Exodus 19—20). They reacted totally differently. They were scared. They not only carried out all the precautions that they were told to, they refused point-blank to go anywhere near God. They begged Moses to represent them. They were terrified.

Seeing God

Terror is the common reaction to any major appearance by God in the Old Testament, even where the experience is mediated by a dream or vision. Look at Isaiah's reaction when he sees God in the temple (Isaiah 6). He is scared stiff, until the angel comes to purify him. Only someone as saintly and down-to-earth as Abraham can meet God face to face without becoming a gibbering wreck (Genesis 18). Hardly surprising, is it? God is holy, separate and righteous. Pure goodness is, in its own way, as frightening as pure evil. It is so much beyond us, we do not comprehend it. We do not measure up. To say it makes us feel inadequate is as obvious as saying that a microbe is smaller than Mount Everest.

All this is fair enough. We are not fit to stand in the presence of God. His light makes us see how dark we are. Should we, then, get depressed and wallow in our sin? What do you think?

Why did God appear to the Israelites on Mount Sinai? It was not to condemn them but to show them how to get closer to him. Again and again throughout the Bible we are told that God does not want to condemn anyone (for example, Hosea 11). We seem surprisingly happy to condemn ourselves but he stands there offering us a way out, first through the way of life given to his people Israel, then through Jesus.

Was Jesus the non-scary encounter with God? Actually, he did scare quite a lot of people—people with something to lose. The people he did not scare were the ones most likely to run away from glowing clouds, the not-very-good people with *nothing* to lose—like many of us. Sometimes shock tactics work; sometimes a more gentle way works. God uses both.

We cannot take the day off work to go and hear Jesus preach. He has not been around in the flesh for two thousand years. You may have heard stories about him turning up to visit people since then but they are few and far between and probably do not happen to people like us, any more than the *Shekinah* invades our bedrooms.

We have to get on with our lives on our own and, in truth, we may well be grateful for that. Things are much less disturbing that way. We do not like being disturbed—but we may need it.

Let me in

To be fair, there are really three types of people: those who just do not want to be disturbed by God at all; those who say they want God in their lives but at a subconscious level would really rather be left alone; and those who do desperately want God in their lives right here, right now. Funnily enough, the things I am about to say about the presence of God apply to all of them without much variation, because no matter what we want, we all need the same thing—God; in our lives; now.

You probably know the passage from Revelation that begins, 'Behold, I stand at the door and knock…' (Revelation 3:20). (Again, God is expressing his desire not to condemn, in spite of the sin of those he is talking to.) You have probably also seen Holman Hunt's painting 'The Light of the World' which is based on that passage. It is a painting I have always rather liked because of its odd, other-worldly lighting, but in many ways it is a very genteel picture. Christ holds up his lantern and gently taps at the overgrown door. Apparently the model for Christ was female because Holman Hunt could not find a male face he thought suitable. No provincial carpenter, this. You wonder if anyone would hear him knocking.

Personally, I think the painting has it all wrong. Jesus is not timorously tapping at the door but hammering at it so loudly that it is deafening. Perhaps we mistake the noise for thunder but he wants to get in. And when he says he is coming to dinner with us, he does not mean we have to rush down to the chiller cabinet at Marks and Sparks or dig out that old Delia Smith book. No, he has the whole of the angelic catering corps behind him and *he* is throwing the party. (If you don't believe me, how many references can you find in the Bible to the heavenly banquet?)

But Holman Hunt was right about one thing: the only door handle is on the inside. It's our choice. No matter how loudly Jesus knocks, he is not going to bash the door down. We can ignore him if we want to, or shout at him to go away—not that he will. Or perhaps we cannot find the key, or even the door.

Faith and confidence

First we have to convince ourselves that God does want to know us. That comes down to a mixture of faith and evidence. All faith is—or should be—founded on evidence but it is not necessarily the kind you would look for as a scientific proof. Certainly there is evidence all around us, in the fact that so many things come together to allow us not just to exist but also to grow and explore. If the universe was completely irregular, we would never be able to learn anything about it, but it seems to be set up so that we can go from one step to another, learning all the way. But although this may deepen some people's faith, I am not sure that many ever came to faith that way. There are too many possible explanations that do not involve God (though I gather that a high proportion of physicists these days have some kind of faith). C.S. Lewis describes the situation as being more like that of a married man. He does not look for proof that his wife is faithful, because he knows her and that is the most important proof. We know God through a personal relationship. If we do not know him ourselves, we can learn about him through other people's relationships with him.

All right, just because God loves Fred Bloggs and wants to share Fred's life (or rather, wants Fred to share his), it does not categorically prove that he is hammering at *our* door—but it suggests that he might be. And we know that throughout history great sinners have become great saints through meeting God. Saul became Paul. Francis of Assisi went from being a spoiled youth to a truly Christ-like man. Nicky Cruz, in *The Cross and the Switchblade* (Spire Books, 1963), had his life turned around from gang warlord to evangelist. If God loves people like that, why not us? If he can help people like that, why not us?

Nicky Cruz records that his journey was a very rocky ride. Hooray! Other people's 'perfection' can be very dispiriting for the rest of us. Nobody gets an easy ride, least of all saints. But they do seem to be able to live in the presence of God.

Sometimes we regard standing in the presence of God as something that we do after we are dead. We think of all those wonderful pictures of white-robed saints standing around the sapphire throne. It sounds a bit dull, actually, but we confidently believe that praising God face to face is the greatest joy we can achieve. (Is it just me, or does the picture of God hosting the heavenly banquet sound rather more fun? If it is just me, how come the banquet picture is more common in scripture?)

God here and now

The idea of standing in God's presence can be a way of limiting him. We might be able to see God better after we die, but that does not mean he is any less real here and now. If God is God, then he is everywhere and all the time. We can live in his presence continually, not just in the one-off, big, dramatic, earth-shaking moments.

I have always been aware of the presence of God. When I was a small child I did not really know what it was that I was experiencing. Then, when I was eight, I sat in the back of the church and thought, 'You are there, aren't you?' and he was. Ever since, I have been aware of his presence constantly with me.

At least, that is what I tell myself. It is not entirely true. It *is* true most of the time, though I do not go around thinking 'God is with me, God is with me', constantly reminding myself of the fact. He is just there. But sometimes I cannot feel his presence—usually when I am most desperately searching for it. And that experience is frightening. Not to be able to touch God, to feel him there, is to be totally alone in the universe. No amount of human company can ever compensate for that.

Do other people feel like this? I am guessing that they do, although many people will not know God well enough to know what it is that they do not have. They just know there is something missing—something important. To know God and then to be cut off from God—well, one well-known definition of hell is to be confronted by God and know that you have cut yourself off from him.

So if God is ever-present, why do we feel cut off from him and what can we do about it? How do we get the pillar of fire back into our lives? How do we follow him out of the desert?

Problems

As is often the case, the first step is to define the problem. One reason could be illness. Anything that clouds the brain and distorts the perceptions could be a cause. Our relationship with God is largely mediated through our mind. Any mental illness or physical ailment that affects mental states can get in the way. If you have any reason to suspect that this is the problem, go to your doctor. There is no shame in being ill. If you have had an illness diagnosed, accept it and whatever treatment is offered. It may be necessary to accept an impediment in your relationship with God so long as you are ill. If this is the case, keep reminding yourself that it is not your fault. Faithfulness that does not seem to make a difference in the world is just as precious to God as that which overflows with results. It may be a frustrating situation but all is not lost.

Of course there is no harm in trying to improve things. Prayer always comes top of the list, even if it does not seem as if anyone is listening. It might be an idea to try different types of prayer and meditation to see if you can find one that gets through—or rather, one that helps you to hear the answer. A little creative thought about alternatives may be helpful in itself and provide you with a workable solution.

One obvious barrier is sin. This is not a word that anyone wants to hear but it's something that everyone indulges in. There are times—

for some people, their whole lives—when we try to dig a trench between ourselves and God. We may know what we are doing, we may not. There are times when I have keenly wished that God would go away and let me get on with my life. Not for ever—but did he have to be quite so holy, right at this moment? I just want to indulge myself a little. I have other things to do.

For most people, it is not the big sins that cause the problems. It is a constant accumulation of little sins. Selfishness, bad temper, a harsh word here and ignoring a neighbour there. We all do it every day. More than likely, we sin most by omission. We cannot be bothered or we fail to notice a need we could fulfil. We are too busy to spend five minutes chatting to someone who needs a kind word. It gets to be a habit, doing the wrong thing and not doing the right. And then we wonder where God has gone in our lives.

I sometimes wonder if it is not easier to recover from big sins because they are so much more noticeable.

The world's way

If these little sins are the problem, the first thing we need to do is wake up. We tend to assume it is all right to live down to the world's standards. We are just doing what everyone else does. We are not so bad. I mean, we're not meant to be perfect, are we?

I suspect you will already know the answer to that one. Jesus did say that we are meant to be perfect, even as our Father in heaven is perfect (Matthew 5:48). To be fair, perfect in that context should be translated as something like 'fit for the job', but that is enough in itself. More specifically, Jesus talked about not living down to the world's standards when we decide to whom we should do good (for example, Luke 6:32–36). If we are only nice to people who are nice to us, well, everybody does that, don't they? That is merely self-interest or at best the cosy feeling we get from being with 'our kind of people'. Love your enemies. Even harder, love those you are just not interested in.

The long and the short of it is to be more aware. Our sensitivities have been dulled by looking at the world for so long and not looking at God. We need to pick up on what we need to do to be like God, because it is only when we are like him, when we are truly his children, that we are able to see him clearly. You might call this the opposite of a vicious circle. The more we see God, the more we can be like him; the more we are like him, the more we see him.

All this might seem to be concentrating too much on works rather than faith, on what we do rather than what God does. On the other hand, James said that faith without works is dead (James 2:17). And there is nothing more useless than a dead faith—not one that is lost, because that can be re-found, but one that is full of the dust of technicalities rather than the fire of love. What we do is an expression of our love; it is an expression of who we are.

Leading on from this, is it sometimes true that we cannot be bothered? We know that if we let God in, he will shake up our lives like a hurricane. There are numerous examples of this in the Bible. It happens right the way through the Old Testament, from Noah onwards, to Abraham, David, Jeremiah, Ezekiel. This shaking is probably the single most common experience in the New Testament —the disciples, Martha and Mary, Cornelius. For them, life would never be the same again.

But mostly we like our lives. We shaped them. They may not go exactly as we wanted but we can manage a good approximation—and that is true even for many people going through the wilderness. There are very few whose lives are totally at odds with what they wanted for themselves. Let God in and anything might happen. Let God in and we might end up as hero or saint. Do we want that? No, mostly we do not.

So we shut him out, settling for half measures. We do what we think God ought to want, rather than what we suspect he does want. We keep our heads down. 'The trivial round, the common task, should furnish all we ought to ask.' We might abhor that sentiment in principle, but in practice we are far more comfortable with it than we are with the great adventure. We try to box God in, then we wonder why we do not see him.

The answer is fairly obvious. Invite God back into your life to do what he wants. Then be prepared to take the consequences. And remember, God is the source of all virtues, including courage. Ask and you shall receive. Because underneath, under all that uncertainty and wanting to stick with what we know, aren't we really in two minds? In spite of what I have just said, don't we all have the sneaking feeling that we would like to be the hero?

When you stop seeing

There is a problem that may have affected the Israelites—did they end up taking God for granted?

They did, after all, have an unmistakable sign of his presence with them day and night for forty years. Anything that sticks around for that long becomes part of the furniture. You hardly notice it any more. You do not miss it until it is gone, like a building scheduled for demolition. It is amazing what you can end up not seeing if it is around for long enough, even people. A moving, glowing cloud would be no different.

It is true that the pillar of cloud signalled when the Israelites should move and when they should stop, but I suspect that in people's minds this may have made it more of a traffic signal than a message from God.

Do we take God for granted? We do not have such a big visual reminder, although we do have reminders, of course. I come from a city where the most obvious sight is the cathedral. It is the biggest building in the city, perched right on top of the hill. It can be seen from almost anywhere outdoors. On a clear day you are supposed to be able to see it from forty miles away. Yet I have been seeing it all my life and unless the light is particularly spectacular or unusual I can look right at it without noticing it. Jesus said that a city set on a hill cannot be hidden (Matthew 5:14). What he failed to mention is that it can be ignored.

Do you ignore God? Not deliberately, but because the signs of his presence have become so familiar? Encountering God has been compared to marriage. You fall in love. You have a honeymoon period when everything is zingy. Things start to settle down—after all, you cannot go around with your head in the clouds all the time. Then you either settle into a companionable, loving relationship, coping with the ups and downs, or you stop talking and start taking each other for granted. And we all know what happens to a marriage when people stop talking. God never drifts away from us but we can drift away from him.

Can we get back that first flush of love? In the relationship with God, there is no such thing as an irretrievable breakdown. We can always come back and he will welcome us with open arms. It will not be exactly the same as it was before. With any luck it will be stronger.

How? How do we do that? All of us need, to some extent, to make that return, because we have moved away. No two people will have exactly the same answer because no two people are exactly the same or have the same relationship with God. However, one thing is the same for everyone—you have to want it.

And that is virtually a guarantee that you will get it ('Ask and it will be given to you', Matthew 7:7). It may be a long, hard slog—very few things worth having are easily obtained—but we will find God because he wants to be found. He will *always* respond to our search, even to our weakest expressions of love. He will guide us to him in the best possible way, although 'best' means 'most complete' and not necessarily 'easiest'.

Prayer, again

The obvious place to look for a way back to God is through prayer. Yes, prayer again, though this time it *is* obvious. To go back to the marriage analogy, can you have a successful relationship if you are not talking to each other? If you go out to look for someone, you call out to them.

Prayer can be hard. It is a discipline. We need to keep at it if we are going to get anywhere. The more we do it, the easier it becomes. The more we do *not* do it, the easier it is to skip it. If prayer is hard, you might need to experiment. Use written prayers rather than trying to think up your own words, or vice versa. Meditate, or join a prayer group or prayer triplet. Prayer is something that can be adapted to fit you and your relationship.

God in the world

Try looking for God in other people. We are all made in his image so we can all show that image to each other. He may use us to drop an appropriate word to someone else. You do not have to be a preacher to do that! And God, being God, can show himself through others in many different ways.

He can show himself through others as they serve us but, perhaps more importantly, he can show himself as we serve them. The God who suffers with us is most obvious in the weak rather than the strong, and as we serve we open up our hearts and find that he is already within us. At best it will not only restore our faith but build it beyond our wildest dreams.

Another place we are meant to find God is in Communion. That is what the name means. This is a good place for me to repeat that not everything works for every person. The Communion service has never done much for me. I take Communion as often as I can, because you are 'supposed' to, but I tend to get more from the sermon than the sacrament. I feel vaguely guilty about this, as if I *ought* to get something out of it, but the only time that happened was the one time I administered the wine. I felt God's presence very powerfully. I also felt extremely nervous!

Should I feel guilty that I do not feel much? No, I do not think so. Just because Communion means so much to other people, just because it is a traditional means of grace, that does not mean it has to work for me. I am not other people. God has different ways of speaking to me.

God will speak to you in the way most appropriate for you. Spending too much time worrying about why he is not speaking in one way rather than another may lead you to miss the message altogether.

Try taking Communion on a regular basis and see if you meet God there. But if that or any other suggestion does not work, it is no big deal. There is always another way through.

Theology—thoughts about God

It goes without saying that you should read the Bible if you want to know about God but it might also help to read some theology. Some people grow up with unhelpful beliefs about God—who he is and what he does—that may get in the way of being able to meet him. If you turn up at a train station looking for a tall, blond man and he turns out to be a small, dark woman, it is no wonder if you miss each other. God knows what you are like but if you think he is something other than he is, you might still be looking for someone else, even when he is tapping you on the shoulder. Indeed, if you do not know who *you* really are, who you are in God's eyes, you could still miss him. It is as if you do not know what your real name is, so when he calls you by it, you do not respond.

Try reading other people's thoughts to see if they can add anything to your own. Your reading can be academic or popular—anything with a good reputation that suits the position you find yourself in. Perhaps you will even begin to see where God has stepped into your life in the past. Then maybe you can see where he is taking you in the future. If you can manage that, you will be doing better than I am.

Finally, it might be helpful to set up some visual reminders of God's presence in your life. What they are will be personal to you. A cross is obvious but something that reminds you of an event in your life may be more effective—an event where you know God's presence was real for you. You just need something that you can glance at and think, 'Oh, yes…'. It might also be an idea to change your visual aids regularly, so that you do not stop noticing them. God sets a lot of reminders along our way, just like the pillar of fire. We do ourselves a favour if we take time to observe them, because they are there to lead us to our Promised Land.

CHAPTER 12

CROSSING THE JORDAN

Messing up

Read Numbers 13—14.

In the beginning there was no need for the Israelites to spend forty years in the desert. What God wanted was that they should pass straight over into the Promised Land. I expect that that is what the Israelites themselves wanted but they messed up in a big way and got themselves stranded, so badly stranded that a whole generation of them would never see the good life that God had in store for them.

What about us? Each of us at some time reaches the point where we can get out of the desert. We tend not to believe that. In my experience, we believe that whatever condition we are in will last for ever but circumstances and our response to them change constantly. One day we will have the chance to get out of the desert. Will we take it?

The answer might seem to be a fairly obvious YES! But look at the Bible text. The Israelites know what they have been promised—a land flowing with milk and honey. The spies report back that that is exactly what it is, an earthly paradise (Numbers 13:27). They even bring back an enormous bunch of grapes—which is now the logo of the Israeli Tourist Board! The land has everything they could want.

But they are too scared to go and claim it. Everything has been set up for them, but they will not take the final step. Only Joshua and Caleb are prepared to trust in God, and only they eventually reap the benefits—half a lifetime late because of other people's behaviour.

We wouldn't do that, would we?

The truth is, much as we hate our wilderness prison, it can be a great deal more comfortable than the unknown future. We know where we are in the wilderness. We know how things work here. We have the comfort of familiarity. It can even have certain advantages. We might be relieved of responsibilities. We might not have to take decisions. We might get sympathy and help that we never had before.

I can think of several things that would change if I got well. For a start, my weekly income would be just about halved as I went from one set of benefits to another. I would have to go back to the continual round of rejection that is job-seeking. And I would have to start driving again. I hate driving—it scares the living daylights out of me—and I was very glad when I had a genuine reason to give it up. If I get well, I might be able to avoid it a lot of the time but I would have to relearn and use the skill occasionally—not something I want.

There are many other things that could change in less easily predicted ways. Relationships, for instance. How will people behave towards us if they know we no longer have the problem we used to have? Do we even use our wilderness to manipulate others? 'You have to be nice to me because…'; 'I can't be there for you because…'; 'It's not my fault, it's…'. That is very much of a subconscious, if not a conscious, temptation.

So we do not take the opportunity, or else we deliberately do not see it. Fear or familiarity or laziness keep us where we are. It might be too much effort to make the change so we carry on leading half-lives. And like atomic half-lives, they get less and less and less.

If that is what you want, there is nothing I or anyone else can do for you. But I do not think that that is what most people want, not really. They just need a little encouragement (or maybe a big push). They need to be able to see the way out, though often it will be fairly clear—if not neon-lit, then at least sporting glow-in-the-dark paint.

If the way out is not obvious, then we need to apply the solutions

I have been recommending throughout this book: careful thought to examine the possibilities before us; Bible reading—you never know what you are going to find there; and prayer. Talk to God about it. He might tell you to wait but he will never tell you to give up. He might even show you a door that you can open right away. If you have bothered to read all the way through this book, you might as well try doing something.

Looking in the wrong direction

There is one last problem—running after missed opportunities.

When the Israelites refused to take the chance God offered them, he told them to go back into the desert and stay there for the duration (Numbers 14:20–35). But they did not like the sound of that and decided to follow God's previous plan, despite warnings from Moses. They attacked the Canaanites (Numbers 14:40–45)—not at all clever, although it did work in a backhanded sort of way: many of them did not have to die in the wilderness because they had already got themselves killed on the battlefield.

Some people do waste their lives chasing after the opportunity before last, oblivious to the fact that they can no more catch up with that than with the day it arrived. Both are receding inexorably into the past. And while they are looking backwards, those people cannot see the next chance until it has passed them by. (That might be the definition of a wasted life.) Indeed, they may get themselves into more trouble than they were originally trying to get out of.

We have to take what is offered in the present and never mind that it is different from before. Never mind that it is not exactly what we wanted. Not to worry that we missed one chance and will probably miss the next: if we think like that, we will miss it. I cannot tell you what your chance will be or when it will come—just go for it.

And remember, God—being the loving and merciful God that he is—does not hold our failings and inadequacies against us. He sends us second chances like tube trains. If you miss this one, there is a very good chance there will be another one along in a minute. Jump on board.

Mount Nebo

Read Deuteronomy 34.

There will always be a way out of the wilderness but it might not be
the one we want. We might have to wait a very long time for it and it
may not even be in this life. It depends on what is causing the sense
of exile. Some things we can do something about. Some things have
a natural cut-off point. Some things simply fade away. Others do not.
Illnesses can last a lifetime, though there is always hope that a cure
will be found. Painful situations may never be resolved if that resolu-
tion depends on other people. External circumstances may change
too slowly to be of any use to us. Old age simply happens, though it
need not be a desert place.

We need to differentiate between situations that are being resolved
very slowly and those that are not being resolved at all. It can be hard
to tell the difference when we are on the ground, so to speak: those
situations have many features in common and many of the same
qualities are needed to cope with both. But there is a difference and
it can sometimes be seen. A conventional solution can be worked
towards, hoped for, awaited patiently. If there is no such solution,
things are a little different.

Let me be clear: sometimes the only way out of the wilderness is
death. And no, that does not give the lie to anything I have said about
hope or about exile being temporary. The truth is that our life is a
passing phase and only eternal life, life with God, is permanent. And
that is something to be thankful for.

To non-Christians, or at least to non-religious people, the Christian
view of death probably sounds crazy. Very often, as Christians, we
know these things with our heads but do not believe them with our
hearts. We exhibit the same fears as the rest of the world. So, before
I talk about a lifetime in the wilderness, I will try to restate Christian
beliefs about life and death as clearly as I can.

First of all, life before death is meant to be good. This life was
created by God for us and he loves us. Due to various combinations

of circumstances, it is not as good for most people as it ought to be, but it still can be very good. This life also has a purpose, to get us ready to meet God face to face. This involves loving God, loving our neighbour and loving ourselves in the proper manner, expressed in our actions.

And then we die. But death is not the end. Nor do we come back as another person or hang around as a ghost. Then we *really* start to live. The most common image for this life in the Bible is one big party. The last few chapters of C.S. Lewis' classic story *The Last Battle* give a real feel of it. In that book, Lewis also made two important points: nothing good is ever lost, and heavenly life is more real than this one. We can get a taste of it in this life but too much gets in the way for us to experience it fully. Death is the great clearing away of obstacles. Death puts an end to all pain and grief, as is made clear in Revelation. There will be no more tears (Revelation 7:15–17).

Our access to this heavenly life is made possible by the life, death and resurrection of Jesus, but here is not the place to go into the technicalities of that.

So death is not something to fear but something to look forward to. Of course, I am not recommending suicide! That is not what God wants for us or for the loved ones we leave behind. I can see how someone might feel completely overwhelmed with pain and I am sure God would deal with them mercifully, as he deals with everyone else; but if we are alive, we are alive for a reason.

This, then, ought to affect our attitudes profoundly. We ought to look forward with hope, not fear. Yet I believe that many Christians do look forward with fear.

Why Christians fear death

There could be several reasons for this fear. Spending too much time with the world and not enough with God would be an obvious one. We tend to pick up the attitudes of those around us, and for many people death is absolutely the worst thing because it is a complete termination. If this is the case, try reading the Bible. The idea of life after death—a rather wishy-washy term that suggests ghosts to me—

is not explored in the earlier parts but it is a fact acknowledged by the majority of Jews in Jesus' time. The fact that the Sadducees did not believe in it was seen as remarkable (Mark 12:18–27). Keep reminding yourself of the truth if you have a problem. There may be no objective evidence that there is life after death but neither is there any evidence for anyone else's idea of what happens. If we have found other parts of Christian belief to be reliable, why not this one?

I think the second reason is that some Christians believe all too much in what they fear is waiting for them after death—fire and brimstone. This again comes from a wrong conception of God, a conception that a generation or two ago was regularly propounded by preachers but is now rarely heard from the pulpit. Some people might suggest that preachers have gone too far the other way but still the wrong concept persists.

Yes, God is a God of justice. He hates sin—but he does not hate the person committing the sin. The Bible makes that clear throughout. Ezekiel writes that God told him 'I don't want sinners to die. I want them to stop doing evil so that I can bless them' (Ezekiel 18:23, paraphrased). God is a God of justice but he is also a God of mercy. Why else would he have sent Jesus to suffer in order to save us? So while we ought to be doing our best—with the Holy Spirit's help— to live as if we really are children of God, he is not waiting to zap us every time we slip up.

Some people are just scared of everything. If that is the case for you, you need better help than this book can give. Try going to your doctor or finding a good counsellor. As I have said before, there is no shame in getting help. It is the sensible thing to do.

Forty years in the desert?

Death might not be something to fear but it could be a very long way away. I am in my early thirties. I come from a family where many of my female relations have lived into their eighties and nineties. I think my grandmother is currently going for the record. And that is without adding constantly growing life expectancies. Indeed, some scientists are talking about making us immortal—a wonderful thing if your life is going well (and you do not expect to go to heaven). If life is miserable, the idea is a nightmare.

How do we cope with what might be a very long exile, one we can do nothing about? How did Moses cope? He knew, when the Israelites backtracked from Canaan, that he would never leave the desert, never enter the Promised Land. Daniel and his friends were in a similar situation in Babylon.

Of course we have little evidence of what Moses felt. We can reasonably assume that he was initially depressed at the realization. From the day he saw the burning bush to the day the spies returned with their grapes, he had had one goal in mind. Now he was never going to see that goal fulfilled. It would be natural to assume that he moped for a while.

Some people think that you should be bright and chirpy no matter what has happened. They think that if you are anything else, it is a sign of lack of faith. Fortunately God is more understanding. He knows that we need time to cope with bad news. Sometimes we need time to cope with good news, which can be just as unsettling. He gives us that time, whatever other people might do.

But we cannot mope for ever. Every period of grieving, every period of adjustment, has its own natural termination. Sometimes we might want to extend that period as a defence mechanism or for other reasons, even as a way of controlling others. This is not healthy. We have to get on with life, even if the life we have is very limited. I think that if we examine ourselves honestly, we will know when the time has come to move on.

Patience

When we do move on, one obvious virtue we will need is patience—patience with ourselves, with our circumstances and frequently with other people who do not understand that we are still in the wilderness.

'Oh Lord, give me patience and give it now!' Patience is a virtue that has to be developed. It is part of the fruit of the Spirit (Galatians 5:22) and, like all virtues, it is a gift from God. Also, like all virtues, patience and its reverse are habit-forming. Display patience once and it is easier to do it the next time, and the next and the next and the next. For patience is about *doing*. A patient attitude is not something that just happens, it is an act of will that needs to be put into practice by doing, or deliberately refraining from, the appropriate act.

Sometimes we will need to be patient with God, when he appears to be doing exactly the wrong thing. It may be that we are misreading the situation. It may be that we are attributing something to God that is not part of what he is doing. Fortunately, however, we can be totally honest with God without fear of hurting his feelings or having him retaliate. The latter is not in his nature. As for the former, he does have feelings but he is big enough to take our frustration and loving enough to give us room to get it off our chests.

We need to be patient with other people, many of whom will not understand our problem because they have not been there themselves or are too wrapped up in their own problems to consider ours. (Be honest, have you never done that?) Ideally we should behave better than they do, as Christ taught in the Sermon on the Mount. In practice, we have to keep trying, we have to develop a habit. Sometimes we need to see things from the other person's point of view. Sometimes we just need to bite our lip. We are not going to get out of the wilderness by being rude to people. Indeed, we might push ourselves further in.

Then we need patience with ourselves. We should examine what we can do as well as what we cannot. We are still fundamentally the same people with the same skills and interests. Unless we are in a coma, we can always find something that we can do, something to engage our interest. We can think, we can learn, we can encourage. Life can not only be good, it can be productive if we allow it to be. It might not be as good as we would like but that is true for a great many people, probably almost everyone. It sometimes seems that those who are most challenged are most likely to take up those challenges and make a masterpiece from their life.

Getting the calculations right

There is always hope. Being realistic about our prospects is not the same as looking on the dark side. The unlikely does sometimes happen. Scientists do find cures for diseases. Old age may never be cured but many people are working to alleviate the more distressing side-effects. Circumstances change. Someone new might come into our life or we might find an outlet for talents that we never dreamed of. Our baseline problem might disappear or we might find something else that will turn our life around. We should not be deluded by hope but we should act on the basis of a rational calculation of the odds. Remember, too, that we can never calculate those odds down to the last digit because we do not know all the facts.

Here is an example from *Star Trek*. A group of super-intelligent people has calculated that the Federation will lose a war with billions of casualties. The only alternative is to surrender—that will cost far fewer lives. The Federation will not listen, so the group decides to hand over defence secrets to the enemy in order to bring about a quick and relatively bloodless defeat. When they go to hand over the secrets to the enemy, their plans are foiled when someone releases the Starfleet officer whom the geniuses had taken prisoner in case he talked. They miscalculated on a small thing; they might have miscalculated on a big one. The disaster may not happen. And it might not happen for us, either.

Everyone, Christian or not, should be prepared to die because it will happen one day. That fact is often ignored, despite its obviousness. And death will end all our problems. Nevertheless, our problems could also end before that. People go to fortune-tellers but no one really knows what the future holds—no one except God, and he is not usually telling!

What I am saying is that no problem, no sadness, lasts for ever. It may last a long time, it may last a lifetime. We need to learn to cope with that. We may need to put up with a life we consider only half lived. We may not achieve our goals. What matters is that we do the best with what we have, and in that knowledge we can be content.

Crossing the Jordan

Read Joshua 3—4.

And then the Israelites reached that happy and momentous day when they crossed the Jordan into the Promised Land. All problems solved.

Not quite! The Israelites now faced a completely new set of challenges, several of which they failed to live up to. There was something of a honeymoon period under their new leader Joshua, one of the two spies who had encouraged the people to take the land forty years before. Nevertheless, the Israelites failed to conquer the whole land, they made inappropriate deals with the locals and they very soon fell into worshipping idols. They frequently turned their back on God until they needed him to get them out of another crisis.

Just like us.

The challenge of good times

OK, our challenges are different but they are just as real—as real as the ones that we face in the wilderness. If someone on state benefits wins the Lottery, we would not expect all their problems to magically disappear. Some problems would be solved, of course, but they would simply be replaced by others. Instead of the need for money, the Lottery winner might have to cope with demands for money from other people.

Viv Nicholson of 'Spend, spend, spend' fame blames the death of her husband directly on their Pools win. He was killed in a car crash. Previously they had not been able to afford a car.

Certainly some people looking from the outside will assume that once one problem is sorted out, everything goes swimmingly. They may not see the need to offer help or friendship. They may even get jealous. Some will come to understand, given time and patience. Others will not. That, really, is their problem.

A bigger difficulty is our expectations. We sort out what we perceive to be the main problem and we think that all the others should disappear with it. I have done this myself, moving from unemployment to a less-than-perfect job—or from that job to another one.

I am not saying this to depress you. I am not saying that life will be horrible for ever or that every step forward turns into a step back—quite the opposite. What I want to do is to make sure that life in the Promised Land is as good as it can be, rather than being spoiled by chasing rainbows that fade as we reach them.

Again, I am not saying that we should stop following our dreams or looking for something better. The human race would never have got anywhere if that had been its attitude. What I am saying is that the best springboard for those dreams is a full enjoyment of what we have here and now. If we do not appreciate what we have, we are not going to appreciate what we get. And that, surely, is the secret of happiness.

We begin by giving ourselves time to adjust to changes for the better, just as we need to do when something goes wrong. What those changes are will depend on our starting-point but they do not necessarily take us where we were expecting to go. We may simply want everything to return to how it was before. Instead we might be offered something obviously better than what we had—a promotion rather than a simple return to our old job—or we might find the chance of something totally different, like a complete career change.

We do not expect the move from the worse to the better to take guts, but it can. I expect that some of the Israelites were pretty nervous stepping on to the dry riverbed as they crossed the Jordan. No one except Joshua and Caleb was old enough to remember crossing the Red Sea, and this time they did not have a pursuing army at their backs to spur them on. All that water piling up must have been pretty off-putting.

Changed relationships

It probably helped the Israelites that they were in a crowd of their friends and neighbours. We sometimes seem to be on our own. I have already mentioned that many people will not understand our difficulties—many but not all. Some people have the talent to imagine themselves in our shoes. Others will have been in similar situations themselves. Indeed, if you are already in some kind of self-help group, it may be worthwhile starting a follow-up group for those going through a period of adjustment. They often feel they have to leave the group, or may even be asked to leave, because they no longer have the problem with which the group deals! Yet the need for support can be just as great while moving back to normality. Coping strategies and practical tips can be shared, along with emotional support.

Even if there is no such group, it is still worth talking to someone. You may need to do a lot of explaining but many people will have had a similar experience and even those who have not may be keen to help. Wouldn't you if it was the other way round? We do not like to feel we are imposing on someone but it can be quite a compliment to them: it can validate them as a person, by showing that we value what they can do for us. However, coming to rely totally on another person is not healthy for either party.

And of course there is always God, the one who understands our problems better than we do and the one we can never impose upon. He always wants to help.

But talking to anyone, human or divine, may emphasize the fact that our relationships have shifted radically and that we are not the only ones who have to come to terms with our changed circumstances. I mentioned some time ago that because of my illness I am in many ways dependent on my mother. That will change if I get well, bringing a major shift in our relationship. I am not expecting any problems but for some people it might be different. A carer might find their self-worth in the caring role and resent having to give it up. They might not want to share responsibilities or accept help from the person for whom they once cared. And this does not apply only where physical help has been required. We need to be patient rather than pushy, even when we are dying to throw off every trace of our exile.

We also have to understand if our carers seem only too glad to get shot of us. It will have been a strain on them too and perhaps they are looking forward to their new freedom.

Other relationships will change, with friends, colleagues and acquaintances. You might see a lot more of some and a lot less of others. Changes in our own responsibilities may be added. If I get well, I will have to start attending church meetings again, which will bring me back into contact with many people I do not often see at the moment. All those relationships will have to shift slightly.

Perhaps the most important change in relationship will be the change in relationship with myself. Many people in the wilderness find it hard to see themselves as a meaningful adult. They are not effective people. Their contribution does not count, if they feel they can make a contribution at all. They might want to be a responsible adult but when it comes to the crunch it can be hard. It is much less work and much less worry to be a nobody, not to have responsibilities.

On the other hand, some people go too far the other way once they have recovered. They become far too serious and can work or worry themselves back into the desert.

In the desert we ought to learn to be balanced people. We are neither the centre of the universe nor nothing at all. We need to be responsible and hard-working but we also need to learn how to relax and play. We need to put others first without undervaluing our own needs. We need to be both grown-up and child-like, a stage of maturity that by no means everyone reaches.

If we have not learned and developed while we were in the wilderness, we have no reason to think that we will do so once we get out of it. Indeed, we might as well be back in exile. The experience is meant to change us, meant to make us better people—as, indeed, is the whole of life.

What have you learnt?

Life-long learning

I hope you will have learnt something from reading this book—I hope I have learnt something from writing it—but what you have learnt from your life is far more important. What have you learnt today? Do you intend to learn tomorrow? Because we will only learn if we intend to. If we sit at the back of the classroom playing conkers, we will not get much out of the lesson. And the lesson could be fun. It could be fully interactive, multimedia *life*. We were not meant to sit and vegetate. That is when life really gets boring.

So what have you learnt? What have you changed or made plans to change? Changes do not have to be radical. They just have to be right. If you were only slightly off course in the first place, you do not want to go too far in the opposite direction.

We face plenty of challenges ahead, as did the Israelites. A land of milk and honey still needs farming or the cows and the bees will not produce. There is enormous potential in everyone's life but we will still keep running up against the rocks. Finding a job is rarely easy, and neither, in a different way, is giving one up. Finding our own Promised Land takes hard work, soul-searching and a lot of help. But there is a Promised Land across the Jordan, a better life that God wants us to have.

Where have we been? We started out in Egypt, which might have seemed like a good place but was not the right place for us. We moved through the desert, encountering problems and solutions but not necessarily in that order. We messed up and we got things right. And we reached the other side. Did we arrive as changed people? I hope so.

I hope you do reach your own Promised Land. And when you do, I hope you find it within yourself not to fall into the traps of the good times—not to think that it was all your own work any more than the bad times were all your fault; not to think that the world can give you everything you need; not to forget those who need help, nor yet to play Lord or Lady Bountiful to them from your position of superiority. We are all equal in the sight of God and we need to remember that.

We need to remember that our troubles may not be completely over, just because they are over for the moment. And we need not be too bothered by that fact.

We need to remember who we are and who God is.

I promised at the start of this book that I would give a report on my own progress. At the time of writing, my health is no better but

I think I have learnt from writing this book. Certainly I have had to think a great deal and that is never a bad thing. I hope I live up to the things I have written a little better than I did at the beginning.

I hope this book has helped you. If you have any helpful suggestions or comments, I would welcome them. We can all learn from one another and if I ever get to do a second edition or follow-up, you may see your name on the acknowledgments page. Thank you for reading.

Medieval authors often used to end their texts with an elegant request that their readers pray for them. I am not so elegant. Pray for me, as I will pray for you.

www.brf.org.uk

Enter an author, title, subject or phrase

Books ○
Extracts/Info ●

go

brf — Resourcing your spiritual journey

Home
Bible Centre
Book news
Events
Articles
Authors
Who is BRF?

The Bible Reading
Fellowship
First Floor
Elsfield Hall
15–17 Elsfield Way
Oxford
OX2 8FG
England
Tel 01865 319700
Fax 01865 319701
E-mail
enquiries@brf.org.uk

Welcome to BRF

For Bible based resources and information for today's Christian living and for details of all BRF publications, extracts and articles, and a wealth of other information.

Find out about:

▨ New BRF publications

▨ BRF's comprehensive range of resources:
Bible reading and study; Prayer and spirituality; Lent and Advent

▨ BRF authors

▨ Quiet days, Retreats and other events

▨ Barnabas (storybooks, seasonal activity books and teaching resources for 3–11 year olds)

▨ The Barnabas Live Creative Arts and Schools Programme

Visit the BRF website at www.brf.org.uk

BRF is a Registered Charity